Fighter Pilot

World War II in the South Pacific

Fighter Pilot

World War II in the South Pacific

by
William M. Gaskill

Sunflower University Press®
1531 Yuma • P. O. Box 1009 • Manhattan, Kansas 66505-1009 USA

Printed in the United States of America on acid-free paper.

Cover: *Rendezvous Over Bougainville*, by Shigeo Koike, a limited edition fine art aviation historical print, courtesy of Eugene M. Monihan, Concorde Publishing Inc., 4207 Sudley Park Road, Haymarket, Virginia, used by permission. The painting portrays "Operation Dillinger," the successful interception of Imperial Japanese Navy Combined Fleet Commander-in-Chief Fleet Admiral Isoroku Yamamoto, by U.S. Army Air Forces Lockheed P-38 Lightning fighters of the 13th Air Force, over the island of Bougainville, in the Southwest Pacific Theater, on 18 April 1943.

ISBN 0-89745-203-8

Edited by Sandra J. Rose

Layout by Lori L. Daniel

To my family, and my buddies, and all the men and women who fought for our country in World War II, I dedicate this needle's-eye view of World War II, as I saw it in the South Pacific Theater of Operations.

Contents

Foreword

AT SOME TIME every man meets someone who reflects the qualities needed to reach a goal that he, himself, is striving for.

And so it was when I first met Bill Gaskill in the South Pacific, along with his fellow pilots Bob Morriss and Edwin R. Cunningham, Jr. Our common goal was victory in the struggle against the Japanese. As their flight commander-to-be, I chose them to become not just fighter pilots but to become the *BEST* fighter pilots. They did.

Bill, through all the hard training, never shirked from assignments — even volunteering for test flights after planes were serviced.

In spite of the serious times we lived through, there were many humorous experiences. But I'll leave it to Bill to tell them in his own way.

I remember the sight of Bill writing daily in his diary, and writing home nearly every day; so it isn't surprising that he has now accomplished a long-time dream — this book. I feel privileged to be a small part of it.

Chandler P. Worley

P-39 Airacobras in flight. (Photo, D. S. Canning, Maitland, FL)

Preface

I KEPT A DIARY DURING World War II and have been asked many times by my buddies and friends to write about some of my experiences in the Pacific Theater. Because I have been asked, I feel I should speak of the events unfolding and leading up to and throughout the war.

Many veterans are reluctant to dwell on or speak much about that part of their lives. Certainly it is very painful to some and they try to forget it all — which is about impossible. Young people today should know more than I did about our country's history. I once thought history was unimportant, then later was caught up in it — just as each and every reader will become some part of our country's history. Perhaps I can describe this small part of our nation's past in a way that will be interesting.

The South Pacific War Theater of Operations was only one segment of the vast military operation of World War II. I was a fighter pilot and test pilot in the South Pacific with the 347th Fighter Group, 13th Air Force. My task was to escort bombers, as well as conduct dive bombing and skip bombing and strafing of Japanese gun installations, bivouac areas, ammunition dumps, and shipping.

P-38 Lightnings.

Introduction

THIS IS A NEEDLE'S-EYE view of what I saw, heard, read, and experienced while serving my country in the South Pacific in World War II, with excerpts from my day-to-day written record.

I grew up on a farm in Deming, New Mexico. Soon after Pearl Harbor was bombed on 7 December 1941, I signed up for the Army Air Corps. Many of my friends and classmates from Deming had already been shipped out to the Philippines with what had originally been Troop E of the 111th Cavalry of the New Mexico National Guard.

I was accepted as an Air Corps cadet in 1942, and while in the U.S. Army, married my childhood sweetheart, Elvena Ford. I later became a fighter pilot and went to the South Pacific. One of my missions was over the Philippines. In addition to my regular duties, I was the Squadron test pilot and was also on the Aircraft Accident Committee.

When I had joined the 13th Air Force, which was stationed in the South Pacific, much of the combat in our sector was being done by the B-17 and B-24 heavy bombers of the 5th Air Force, and our task was to fly ground support in the Bell P-39 Airacobra, dive bombing and strafing enemy installations, airstrips, gun emplacements, supply depots, bivouac areas, and shipping.

The single-seat P-39 was excellent at low-altitude work,

but its Allison V-1710 engine was "buried" in the fuselage behind the cockpit, and it had only a single-stage turbo supercharger, which rendered it nearly useless against Japanese Zeroes above 17,000 feet. The propeller of the P-39 was driven by a long shaft under the pilot's seat. The intent of the manufacturer must have been to increase the aircraft's maneuverability by putting the engine basically on the aircraft's center of gravity. But it didn't work that way. After 1942, however, the aircraft did make a name for itself as a worthy ground-attack aircraft. And in 1944, the United States sent our P-39s to Russia on the Lend-Lease program. They loved the little plane. As a low-level fighter bomber, it was devastating to the German tanks and mobile equipment, troops, and personnel.

To replace the limited P-39, we received new Lockheed P-38 Lightnings, built for enemy bomber interception — but this plane excelled in all kinds of tasks. Our bombers over enemy targets were being devastated by Japanese fighters. On one mission alone about 30 percent of our bombers had been shot down. The P-38s were called upon to fly cover for them — escort. We would rendezvous over the bombers and accompany them over the target and then back out to sea. After we were out of reach of the Japanese fighters, our Group would form up and leave the bombers to return home. The enemy would be up there all right, but they would not attack as long as the P-38 "fork-tailed devils" were there. We also dive bombed and strafed almost the same as we had in the P-39s. The P-38 was credited with destroying more Japanese aircraft in the Pacific than any other Allied plane.

I flew over 500 combat hours and 177 combat missions in the P-38 and P-39 and believe I am qualified to write on the subject. While overseas, I kept a diary almost every day, and have referred to it frequently in writing this book.

About half of my short two-year military career was spent as a fighter pilot, dive bombing and strafing the enemy. I participated in very little aerial combat. I didn't fly off a carrier, so I don't know much about their operation. That narrows my story down to what I saw from the cockpit of the P-39, then later the P-38, the experiences of my friends, and some research.

Chapter 1

In the Beginning

IN 1916 — five years before I was born — the Mexican revolutionary leader Pancho Villa raided Columbus, New Mexico, which is about 25 miles south of our farm in Deming. Sixteen American citizens were killed. This caused quite a stir, and a week later, General John J. Pershing led a "punitive" expedition to Mexico with 10,000 men.

The telegraph operator of the El Paso Southwestern Railroad frantically tried to call General Pershing at Fort Bliss in El Paso, Texas. The Mexicans shot out her light; a piece of glass cut her on the neck. She then grabbed her baby and ran upstairs and placed it under the bed. Running back downstairs and without the light, she again alerted General Pershing that they were under attack.

After reaching the General, she ran upstairs and got her baby, went outside and took a serape off of a dead Mexican soldier, wrapped herself and her baby in it, and ran to the hospital to receive treatment.

The Army was called out, and eventually a third of our standing military pursued Pancho Villa's forces into Mexico. Incidentally, it was the first time the United States Army had taken airplanes to war against an enemy, primarily for scouting purposes. It was also the first time our mechanized cavalry was used to reconnoiter into another country. They never did catch up with Pancho Villa, but it was good troop training prior to World War I.

The First World War began 28 July 1914, between Austria-Hungary and Serbia. One month prior to that was the spark that had caused the war, the assassination of Austrian Archduke Ferdinand in Sarajevo, Bosnia, igniting the bonfire of fears of invasion amongst the major powers — Austria-Hungary, Germany, Russia, France, and Britain. But the Austrians did not really understand the complexities of European power politics, and so their ultimatum to the Serbs (South Slavs) led to threat of Russian intervention and a chain reaction amongst the powers.

And today we are in the same location with some of our forces — a cause for worry, that history could repeat itself if the world's leaders are not mindful.

World War I escalated into a global war involving 32 nations; 28 nations were called the Allies, the other four were the Central Powers. Austria declared war on Serbia; then on 1 August 1914, Germany declared war on Russia. On 3 August, Germany declared war on France, and then Britain declared war on Germany. But the United States did not enter the war until April 1917; the Armistice was signed by the Allied and Central Powers on 11 November 1918.

While growing up in New Mexico after World War I, I didn't pay much attention to history; it seemed boring and unimportant. I didn't know anyone involved with the military or anyone contributing to the defense of our country. But today I see a need for our young people to know more about world events, and we need to keep better prepared than we were back then. Our leaders must not let us be drawn into civil and tribal wars that are never going to be settled.

In 1939, I joined the Horse Cavalry, Troop E, 111th Cavalry, of the New Mexico National Guard, as did many other Deming boys. That was the "in" thing to do at the time. Guard service was a diversion for us with its monthly meetings and yearly encampments. Before World War II, we thought going on maneuvers was fun. The well-bred, high-spirited horses of our Cavalry Troop were different from our old plow horses down on the farm. I remember that at encampment I had to walk the picket line at night. This is far different from what a picket line is today. Then the horses were all tethered to a long rope line between trees. They were not allowed to lie down the entire two weeks of encampment. I had to walk up and down the line and keep them all standing. If one horse lay down, another would probably soon step over his tie rope, with a resulting pandemonium.

Sometimes the order would come quickly to saddle up, pack up, and move out because the "enemy" was coming. We would try to find all of our gear and our horses in the dark — what confusion. Later on these games became real to some of these men after they were sent to the Philippines.

In 1940, when we were ready for our annual encampment, I couldn't go because my dad was ill and I had to stay and help on the farm. When I told the officials, they said that if I couldn't go I would have to get out of the Guard. The other boys went to camp; but instead of returning home, they were sent on to Fort Bliss in El Paso, Texas, where they underwent intensive training and were converted to the 200th Coast Artillery in April 1941. In the fall of 1941 they were sent to the Philippines.

I met the train as it came through Deming with the men on their way overseas. They couldn't even get off, and it was a sad day for everyone. Shortly after our boys arrived in Manila, Pearl Harbor was bombed, and I went down and signed up for the U.S. Army Air Corps.

Chapter 2

Chronology of World War II

1931 — Japan took over Manchuria.

1937 — Japan began to take over China, occupying their main ports. We went to the aid of China with the P-40 War Hawks of the American Volunteer Group (AVG) hired by General Claire L. Chennault under General Chiang Kai-shek. The AVG flew these planes against Japanese bombers.

1938 — Adolf Hitler, head of Germany's National Socialist Party, annexed Austria; Benito Mussolini, of Italy, supported him. Hitler had always been unhappy with the Versailles Treaty of World War I, which put a heavy burden on Germany to repay its war reparations — even though we didn't enforce the terms. He began aggression all over Europe, taking over part of Czechoslovakia. By then, he had built up his armies.

1939 — On 23 August, the Nazi-Soviet Pact was signed in Moscow giving Joseph Stalin a free hand in Finland, Estonia, Latvia, eastern Poland, and eastern Romania.

Hitler seized the remainder of Czechoslovakia and on 1 September marched into Poland. Many military officers and others were executed. Waves of German bombers smashed railheads and other strategic targets. That country fell.

May 1940 — By this time, Hitler had conquered Denmark, Norway, Holland, Belgium, and Luxembourg, and had pushed into France. He had previously signed non-agression pacts with different countries, but he honored almost none of them. The British and French troops were pushed to the coast at Dunkirk where a heroic rescue effort took place. Hundreds of British (and some French) ships and boats of all descriptions slipped in, carrying 338,226 French and British troops across the English Channel to Britain. But thousands of people left behind were slaughtered on that beach in France.

June 1940 — France surrendered to Germany. In May, Winston Churchill had become Prime Minister of Great Britain. Britain desperately needed the help of the United States. President Franklin D. Roosevelt vowed not to send troops to Europe; but in March 1941, he would initiate the Lend-Lease program to provide food, munitions, and other goods to Britain and then to Russia. The Lockheed P-38 Lightning airplanes were being developed to intercept and shoot down German bombers, which by this time were brutally pounding England. Coventry, England, was almost destroyed by bombs, but the British people stubbornly hung on.

April 1941 — Hitler moved against Greece and Yugoslavia. General Erwin Rommel, of Germany, launched a successful counteroffensive against the British in Libya.

June 1941 — In 1939 Hitler had signed an agreement with Russia that he would not declare war against her and gave her a free hand in part of Poland and some other countries. But on 22 June 1941, Germany did invade Russia, with about three million troops on a 2,000-mile front, and Russia declared war. Having just conquered Yugoslavia and Greece, where British forces were aiding the Greeks, Hitler was concerned about the closeness of the British airfields to the Ploesti oil fields in Romania; oil was a vital and necessary ingredient in Hitler's war plan. Germany took country after country. It also wanted to drive the British out of northern Africa and gain control of the Suez Canal and the oil fields nearby in Arabia.

Hitler would not listen to his generals who knew more about the logistics of war and the chances of winning or losing a battle than he did. He simply ordered them on to conquer more and more territory. Later, as things went wrong in Russia throughout the winter, he flew into rages.

7 December 1941 — The Japanese launched air attacks on Pearl Harbor, Guam, and Wake Island as its navy bombarded Midway Island; the United States declared war on Japan the following day.

11 December 1941 — Germany and Italy declared war on the United States. General Rommel had made great strides in northern Africa.

January 1942 — The Japanese entered Manila in the Philippines, then swept down the Malay peninsula and captured Singapore and Java.

11 March 1942 — President Roosevelt ordered U.S. Army General Douglas MacArthur to go to Australia to lead the Pacific Command from there. He vowed to return to the Philippines.

9 April 1942 — On the Bataan peninsula, U.S. Army Major General Edward King surrendered to the Japanese Imperial Army.

18 April 1942 — General James H. "Jimmy" Doolittle led a surprise bombing attack on Tokyo from the carrier USS *Hornet* to shock the Japanese out of their complacency.

6 May 1942 — In Corregidor, Lieutenant General Jonathan M. "Skinny"

Wainwright surrendered the rest of our troops in the Philippines; Mandalay and Burma also fell to the Japanese.

7 and 8 May 1942 — The Battle of the Coral Sea was a turning point in which the Japanese were stopped in their aggression in the Pacific. This was the first time in history that no warships fired on each other — only airplanes against other airplanes and ships.

4 and 5 June 1942 — Japan tried to capture Midway Island north of Hawaii. It ended in a decisive victory for the United States. Again, only aircraft engaged. After the U.S. sank four Japanese carriers and their complement of planes, they turned and headed for Japan. At about the same time, General Rommel continued to make great strides in northern Africa, capturing Tobruk, and driving into Egypt within striking distance of the Suez Canal; the United States readied troops for an invasion of French North Africa.

July 1942 — Hitler's Sixth Army and Fourth Panzer Army were advancing toward Stalingrad.

7 August 1942 — U.S. Marines landed on Guadalcanal in the Solomon Islands and fought a six-month bloody battle. It was the beginning of our retaking the islands of the Pacific. Buna, on the north coast of New Guinea, was also the scene of bitter fighting.

15 September 1942 — Our aircraft carriers the USS *Wasp* and then later the USS *Hornet* were sunk near Guadalcanal as the Japanese tried to retake that island.

September/October 1942 — Germany lost about 200,000 troops trying to hold Stalingrad, in part because of the collapse of the Italian and Hungarian armies.

November 1942 — The United States under General Dwight D. Eisenhower joined British Commander General Bernard Law Montgomery and French troops in battling Rommel's forces in North Africa.

14 December 1942 — Buna, New Guinea, was our first American ground victory against Japan.

February 1943 — The Japanese finally abandoned Guadalcanal!

4 March 1943 — The Battle of the Bismarck Sea, northeast of New Guinea, in which airplanes from the U.S. Army Air Forces (USAAF) and the Royal Australian Air Force (RAAF) sank 10 Japanese warships and 12 transports loaded with Japanese replacement troops. We lost only two bombers and three fighter aircraft.

18 April 1943 — Japanese Admiral Isoroku Yamamoto was shot down by Major John W. Mitchell's P-38s of the 339th Fighter Squadron, 347th Fighter Group, 13th Air Force, near Bougainville in the Solomons.

13 May 1943 — The German and Italian armies were defeated in North Africa.

23 May 1943 — Attu, in the Aleutians, was recaptured by the United States after a three-week battle beginning this day. The Japanese had occupied part of these islands off the coast of Alaska for about a year.

June 1943 — U.S. forces recaptured Rendova Island in the Solomons.

July 1943 — The Allies invaded Sicily and then went on into Italy where the Americans lost 70,000 men. Italy surrendered in September 1943, and by then U.S. planes were bombing the Ploesti oil fields in Romania.

September 1943 — General MacArthur's forces captured Salamaua and Lae, New Guinea.

21 November 1943 — Tarawa, in the Gilbert Islands, was retaken from the Japanese in bitter fighting.

November 1943 — President Roosevelt and Prime Minister Churchill met with Stalin in Teheran to plan a cross-Channel military attack, giving it the code name OVERLORD. It was originally set for May 1944.

January 1944 — Russia entered Poland and executed thousands of Polish officers and civilians, including women and children. There were mass killings of Jewish prisoners at the Auschwitz concentration camp by the Nazis.

February 1944 — U.S. Marines landed on the Marshall Islands. This was prewar Japanese territory (the Kwajalein Atoll). The Central and Northern Pacific Naval campaigns were conducted by Admiral Chester W. Nimitz.

6 March 1944 — U.S. B-17 Flying Fortress and B-24 Liberator bombers dropped 2,000 tons of bombs over Germany.

12 April 1944 — Americans lost 2,000 planes in air battles over Germany.

22 April 1944 — General MacArthur landed on Hollandia, Dutch New Guinea.

April 1944 — British troops regained almost all of New Britain Island in the Bismarck Archipelago except Japan's large supply base at Rabaul.

27 May 1944 — MacArthur's troops landed on Biak Island; airfields there would provide a base for U.S. B-24 Liberator long-range bombers.

6 June 1944 — D-DAY for the war in Europe. American, British, and Canadian troops numbering 155,000 landed in Normandy (the coast of France) with 4,000 ships and 3,000 airplanes under Allied Supreme Commander General Dwight D. Eisenhower, to drive the Germans back along a 100-mile front. The Allies suffered 40,000 casualties in the first week. By the end of June, there were 850,000 men and 150,000 vehicles ashore.

14 June 1944 — American amphibious forces invaded Saipan in the Marianas only 1,500 miles from Japan.

19 and 20 June 1944 — The Battle of the Phillipine Sea was conducted under Admiral Marc A. Mitscher and his U.S. Task Force 58.

July 1944 — Japanese Premier General Hideki Tojo, chief of the army general staff, was relieved of command after he admitted "disaster in Saipan."

25 July 1944 — U.S. Army General Omar N. Bradley finally broke through the German lines at Normandy, with the help of U.S. General George S. Patton's Third Army, General Courtney H. Hodges's First Army, General Alexander C. Patch's Seventh Army, and the Fifth and Ninth Armies. At about this time, Germany used the flying V bomb, called the buzz bomb, on London creating quite a nuisance and causing some casualties. It had no pilot but had a rocket engine.

10 August 1944 — U.S. Marines quickly followed up the victory on Saipan by taking Tinian and establishing a beachhead on nearby Guam.

25 August 1944 — General Patch and General Patton closed in, and the German troops in Paris surrendered to French General Philippe Leclerc. Allied Forces were closing in on Germany; and Romania (on 23 August) and Bulgaria (on 9 September) surrendered to the Russians.

16 September 1944 — 5,000 Allied planes pounded Germany.

September/October 1944 — U.S. troops landed in the western Carolines at Peleliu and Ulithi and Ngulu.

20 October 1944 — General MacArthur returned to the Philippines, landing on the island of Leyte with 100,000 U.S. troops.

23 through 25 October 1944 — The Japanese navy retaliated in the Battle of Leyte Gulf but lost two battleships, four cruisers, four carriers, and nine destroyers. Thirty-six Japanese warships were sunk against six of ours. American losses included the aircraft carrier USS *Princeton.*

5 November 1944 — USAAF B-29s from India bombed Singapore and Sumatra; and a raid on Manila, on Luzon, the main island of the Philippines, destroyed 440 Japanese planes on the ground. Japanese troops in China forced us to retreat from some of the Chinese American bases.

24 November 1944 — 20th Air Force B-29s bombed Tokyo.

December 1944 — U.S. troops landed on Mindoro Island, Philippines. At the Battle of the Bulge in Ardennes, on the French-Belgian border, the enemy penetrated Allied lines 45 miles deep and 60 miles wide, but was held by General Montgomery's British on the north and thrown back by the U.S. First Army and General Patton's Third Army on the south. Patton then took Frankfurt, Germany, and moved toward Berlin 198 miles away. Allied Forces captured over 300,000 German troops in two weeks.

January 1945 — On Luzon, we made a landing 100 miles north of Manila. After three weeks of heavy fighting and losses, the Japanese were finally driven out, but hard fighting continued at Mindanao, the second largest island of the Philippines at the south end of the group, and at Luzon.

February 1945 — 90 USAAF B-29 Superfortresses of the 20th AF bombed Tokyo.

19 February through 16 March 1945 — U.S. Marines took Iwo Jima (part of the Volcano Islands), in the Western Pacific, directly south of the Bonin Islands, but we sacrificed 6,800 American lives and 19,000 wounded.

1 April 1945 — American troops invaded Okinawa in the Ryukyus, 360 miles south of Japan; there the Japanese kamikaze (suicide) pilots were used against our forces, sinking 15 naval vessels and damaging 200. Admiral Nimitz wanted to proceed and invade Japan, but General MacArthur's strategy, which prevailed, was to invade the Philippines first.

12 April 1945 — President Franklin D. Roosevelt died and Vice President Harry S. Truman took over.

28 April 1945 — Italy's Mussolini, his mistress, and 16 Fascist henchmen were executed by their own countrymen, when they realized that Fascism had been defeated.

30 April 1945 — Adolf Hitler, together with his mistress Eva Braun, and Josef Goebbels, along with his family, committed suicide. Berlin fell to the Russians.

8 May 1945 — German General Alfred Jodl, Admiral Karl Doenitz, and Field Marshal Keitel surrendered Germany to the Allied Forces. — Victory in Europe, V-E Day!

26 May 1945 — Tokyo was nearly destroyed by bombs and fire storms.

June 1945 — Australian troops invaded Borneo and Brunei Bay, on the northwest coast of Borneo. The Battle of Okinawa finally ended on 21 June with 12,000 killed and 30,000 wounded in the sea, land, and air conflict. U.S. Army General Simon B. Buckner was among those killed. Japanese casualties were about 100,000 military, plus that many more civilians. Our aircraft carrier USS *Bunker Hill* suffered 373 deaths from a kamikaze plane. To date, 7,800 Japanese aircraft had been lost to our 736. By the end of the war, 5,000 kamikaze pilots had died, but we lost 34 American warships from these attacks.

July 1945 — General MacArthur announced the liberation of the Philippines from the Japanese. The United States made a direct appeal to Japan to quit the war or face total destruction. Over 600 bombers blasted a Japanese naval base. The Japanese formally rejected the call to surrender.

6 August 1945 — President Truman authorized, and the USAAF dropped, the atomic bomb on Hiroshima, Japan.

9 August 1945 — A second atomic bomb was dropped on Nagasaki.

14 August 1945 — With both cities virtually destroyed, Emperor Hirohito announced to his people the defeat of Japan and agreed to unconditional surrender.

2 September 1945 — Military leaders led by General MacArthur signed the documents of surrender on board the battleship USS *Missouri*. General Wainwright, Admiral Nimitz, and Admiral Robert B. Carney were among the dignitaries there to sign, along with many heads of state. General MacArthur, who became the military governor of occupied Japan, established headquarters in Yokohama and returned to the Philippines as he had promised; but his flamboyance and arrogance was a constant irritation to the new President, Harry Truman.

Chapter 3

Japanese Aggression in the Pacific

AS THE WAR PROGRESSED IN Europe, early in 1941 the Japanese complained that the Americans, British, Chinese, and Dutch — the ABCD Command — were blockading their country. The Japanese Imperial Forces were building a successful war machine and needed oil, rubber, and other raw materials, which came out of the countries and islands near southeast Asia like Borneo, Burma, Singapore, and Sumatra, owned or controlled by the British and Dutch.

In 1937, the U.S. had told Japan to get out of

China, but instead, in Nanking, as in other cities, they lined up thousands of Chinese — old men, women, and children — and shot them in the back of the head. There were 40,000 killed in Nanking alone. Those that could work had already been selected for slave labor in mines and factories. The Chinese had no weapons whatsoever to defend themselves. The Japanese bombed them mercilessly.

And that was when the Flying Tigers of the American Volunteer Group — the AVG — had come into the picture, about 1941. The Japanese continued to bomb and pound the defenseless Chinese cities. But by 1942-1943, the AVG, under General Claire L. Chennault, began to tear into the bomber formations. Up to that time the Japanese army bombers had felt secure and saw no need to have fighter escorts or even machine-guns on their bombers.

At about the same time, on the perilous Burma Road to India, planes of the AVG caught the Japanese chasing Chinese refugees. The Japanese were strafed and bombed by P-40 airplanes so severely that the whole division fled the scene with what few trucks and equipment they had left. They had been turned back on the only road through Burma over which they had hoped to capture India.

The AVG had accomplished an enormous victory with very few planes. They eventually shot down 300 Japanese aircraft, killing 1,500 air crew, with a loss of only 10 AVG pilots and planes.

Our country later brought supplies into China from India by flying over the Himalayas — The Hump. In this China-Burma-India (CBI) Theater, we lost many planes and pilots, but managed to keep China from collapsing.

When the United States had finally cut off oil and steel shipments to Japan, the Japanese became infuriated. They thought that if they attacked the Americans in the distant Pacific, the U.S. would not retaliate, and the "Rising Sun" could then finish taking over all of Southeast Asia and Australia and the Pacific Islands, including New Zealand. And hence the raid on Pearl Harbor.

". . . A date that will live in infamy" is how President Franklin D. Roosevelt described 7 December 1941. The Japanese Imperial Navy had sailed thousands of miles across the Pacific Ocean with 31 warships and launched over 350 carrier-based planes from 230 miles north of the island of Oahu. These bombers, dive bombers, and fighter planes flew in two waves to make a sneak attack on airfields, shipyards, and other U.S. military installations. They sank four battleships — the USS *Arizona*, USS *Oklahoma*, USS *California*, and USS *Utah* — and badly damaged 12 other warships. Of the nearly 80 craft tied up in the harbor, nearly all were hit, though most of our damaged ships were later raised and repaired. The Japanese planes destroyed around 188 of our planes.

Our casualties were about 2,400 plus half that many wounded. On the USS *Arizona* alone, 1,177 lost their lives. This ship lies where it sank, and is a tomb and memorial. The USS *Oklahoma* was salvaged, but sank in the Pacific, some 400 miles out of Pearl, while in tow to California.

The United States was caught totally by surprise at Pearl Harbor — a brilliant maneuver for the Japanese and a crippling blow for us. It is said that 90 percent of the damage was done in the first 20 minutes of the raid. The whole affair lasted less than two hours. The Japanese pilots were highly trained, well educated, and highly disciplined; many had wartime experience. Some of their leaders had even been educated in the United States. Japanese General Akira Nara was a graduate of the U.S. Army Infantry School at Fort Benning, Georgia. The Japanese lost only 29 planes and 5 midget subs.

The raid was engineered by Japanese Naval Commander and Admiral Isoroku Yamamoto. The commander of the fleet was Admiral Chuichi Nagumo, and the commander of the aircraft mission was Commander Mitsuo Fuchida.

Fuchida wanted to make a third raid, but Admiral Nagumo said "no," and the Japanese fleet turned northwest. Had the Japanese raided our oil and supply depots, our country would have been mortally wounded. One lucky break — our aircraft carriers were all out to sea and thus were not involved.

At almost the same time, the Japanese made air strikes on the Philippines, Wake Island, Guam, Shanghai, and Hong Kong. Later in 1942, they would strike Midway Island, between Pearl Harbor and the Philippines, resulting in a major American carrier victory.

The Japanese had had a long-range strategy. They wanted to establish the "Greater East Asia Co-Prosperity Sphere" in the Western Pacific. And they wanted to achieve all this in six months.

I don't wish to take away from the seriousness of Pearl Harbor and Wake Island, but the ordeal that followed in the Philippines was a terrible and drawn-out affair, resulting in the two worst defeats, then surrenders, in United States history — Bataan and Corregidor.

General Dwight D. Eisenhower had wisely reported to General George C. Marshall that the Philippines, the Dutch East Indies, and China would all be watching us; they might excuse failure, but not abandonment. It seemed that we had committed so much of our war effort to our Allies in Europe that we had simply abandoned the Pacific theater of war. And the loss of our battleships at Pearl Harbor had put us on the defensive so that we couldn't safely get supplies to the Philippines.

The idea behind the Pearl Harbor attack had been to cripple the United States so that we would leave the Imperial Japanese government alone to continue their aggression and conquest throughout the Pacific and Southeast Asia. But on 8 December 1941, the U.S. declared a "state of war" with Japan, and on the 11th, Germany and Italy declared war on the United States.

President Roosevelt addressed the U.S. Congress and the nation:

> Yesterday, December 7, 1941 — a date that will live in infamy — the United States of America was suddenly and deliberately attacked by naval and air forces of the Empire of Japan. . . . Yesterday, the Japanese government launched an attack against Malaya. Last night the Japanese forces attacked Hong Kong. Last night the Japanese forces attacked Guam. Last night the Japanese forces attacked the Philippine Islands. Last night the Japanese attacked Wake Island. This morning the Japanese attacked Midway Island.

Meanwhile, the British were suffering a terrible defeat also. On 10 December 1941, the Imperial Japanese Navy sank two of Britain's best ships, the battleship HMS *Prince of Wales* and the battle cruiser *Repulse,* near Singapore. The British Admiral in charge was of the "old school" and thought he could defeat the Japanese forces without air cover. But he was wrong; naval warfare had changed. Much of the British force was sunk by Japanese bombers and low-flying torpedo planes in a matter of a few hours. Almost all of the rest of the British and Dutch navies there were also sunk by submarines and bombers. Lieutenant General Arthur Percival, commanding British general in Malaya, then surrendered his 70,000 troops to the Japanese.

Subsequently the Japanese turned into savages, attacking in a frenzy, screaming, shooting, bayoneting, raping, and then killing even the wounded in hospitals. So went Christmas Day 1941. The next day, Hong Kong surrendered.

In the Philippines, Japanese bombers and fighter planes attacked Clark Field, near Manila, on Luzon, an old sod field with run-down hangars. The P-40s there were very poorly maintained. The new B-17s had no tail guns and thus were extremely vulnerable to Japanese fighter aircraft. Most of our aircraft were caught neatly lined up on the ground; over half of General MacArthur's Far Eastern Air Force was destroyed. It was almost a second Pearl Harbor.

James Huxtable, a friend from Deming who became a prisoner of war, told me that right after the first bombing of the Philippines on 8 and 9 December, which had knocked out most of our air force there, our boys ran over with cutting torches and removed all the .50-caliber machine-guns from the turrets of the ruined B-17s. This really updated their little arsenal, and they used these guns against the strafing Japanese fighter planes.

What few of our planes that had survived the initial Japanese attack at Clark Field were mostly evacuated from the area and taken south. Looking back, I believe that a well-prepared air force at that particular time would have stopped the Japanese dead in their tracks.

Why did General MacArthur allow his air force to be so vulnerable after we had already been caught at Pearl Harbor? All of the parked P-40s at Clark Field and all but three of the new B-17 Flying Fortress bombers, 30 medium bombers, and observation planes were destroyed in one raid. The Japanese bombing was accurate and deadly. This should be a glaring lesson to our country never again to be so unprepared.

Following the bombing, Japanese General Masaharu Homma began landing troops at Lingayen Gulf, Luzon, Philippines. The newspaper reports in our country were totally distorted and false, claiming big victories for us when, in fact, it was the reverse.

Very quickly General Homma had landed a force in Lamon Bay, 60 miles southeast of Manila. At the time, he had three columns totaling 9,500 skilled troops under his command. In one of General Homma's first encounters on Luzon, his tanks rolled in and fired into a large unit of horses and mules of the U.S. Cavalry. Panic and pandemonium exploded, and almost a complete rout of our forces followed. The main objective of the Japanese was to head south and capture Manila; and in doing so, it was anticipated that all of the Philippines would fall.

Confusion reigned. General Homma had been surprised by how easy it had been to overwhelm us. Yet Jack Lewis, a friend from Deming who was taken prisoner there, stated that in the Philippines Campaign, 20,000 of our own soldiers had held back 250,000 to 300,000 better-equipped Japanese before our obsolete weapons and supplies ran out. Jack spent much of his time in captivity in hospitals.

The men of the Philippine Campaign recalled that when the nurses set up their field hospitals, the cots were in such poor condition that they just crumbled and fell to pieces. And there were almost no medical supplies.

Our troops had obsolete equipment — imagine having horses to defend an area against tanks and mechanized cavalry! Our mortars would blow up; we had guns without some of their parts; only one out of four grenades would work; and torpedoes would be duds. This, along with food shortages, caused morale to plummet. Some of our soldiers had never even practiced firing live ammunition for the sake of economy, and consequently didn't know how to react.

The Philippine civilians and the 70,000 or so Filipino troops were disgusted that the U.S. would abandon them at this time. MacArthur pleaded for help, but none came.

Back at Manila, General MacArthur had decided to set fire to the oil and gas and munitions depots; enough oil and fuel to run our entire fleet for two years was destroyed to keep it from getting into Japanese hands. For some reason we even set fire to our own hangars and airplanes! Then he pulled his troops out and headed south; many of the Filipino troops deserted. The few roads were clogged with retreating civilian refugees and military units — cars, trucks, tanks, carts, and anything to escape the oncoming Japanese.

Our forces were so outnumbered by the Japanese Imperial Army that our Army retreated to Bataan, a peninsula of the island of Luzon, off Manila Bay. The peninsula was 15 miles wide and 30 miles long, and our troops, along with the Philippine troops, had to keep fighting delaying actions to protect those retreating. The terrain was either cut up by steep ravines leading off of the volcanic peaks or it was jungles and swamps. Malaria, dysentery, dengue fever, and starvation took their toll in energy and lives. The soldiers on Bataan had a slogan:

> The battling bastards of Bataan
> No Mama, no Papa, no Uncle Sam

No aunts, no uncles, no nieces
No pills, no planes, no artillery pieces
And nobody gives a Damn.

On 30 December 1941, during this struggle, General MacArthur addressed a small group of people who had gathered on Bataan to inaugurate Manuel Quezon as president of the Philippines for a second term as well as his vice president Sergio Osmena. The battle could be heard in the distance.

Philippine President Quezon was beginning to have doubts and did not want any more bloodshed in his country. But MacArthur kept insisting that U.S. help was on the way.

The Japanese began to encircle our troops, though General Homma's forces had lost many men. But in some of our own outfits, the men were retreating helter skelter. They threw away their guns, their shoes were worn out, they were barefoot, and their clothes were in tatters. Each new line of defense could hold for just a little while.

A Lieutenant Lee wrote:

Saved for another day
Saved for hunger, wounds and heat
For slow exhaustion and grim retreat
For wasted hope and sure defeat.

Major General Jonathan M. Wainwright went to the front lines frequently to encourage his men. He would sit in plain sight for all to see and for the enemy to shoot at. When questioned about this apparently foolish act he replied that he had nothing to offer his troops — no food, no medicine, no help of any kind: "I can only boost their morale." Thus he felt it important to be there.

When General Wainwright's 250 surviving Cavalry horses and 48 pack mules ran out of fodder, he ordered that they be slaughtered for food for the troops, starting with his own horse. For a Cavalry man attached to his mount, this was very traumatic.

But the men of Bataan eventually ran completely out of food, medicine, and ammunition. Our troops there were evidently deemed expendable by the U.S. Army, because by then nearly all of the war effort was being directed to the battle in Europe against Adolf Hitler. General MacArthur retreated and set up headquarters on Corregidor (the rock), hoping to control the entrance to Manila Bay.

It was at this time, on 11 March 1942, that General MacArthur was ordered by President Roosevelt to go to Australia. MacArthur vowed: "I shall return." Most Filipinos trusted General MacArthur and believed, indeed, he would come back. In about three years he did, against great odds.

Meanwhile, General Homma's advance ground to a halt for a short time. The Japanese had regrouped, with about 15,000 fresh troops and about 35,000 "seasoned" men. General Homma was determined to once and for all crush the Americans; Tokyo was putting the pressure on him to end this campaign.

Lieutenant Lee wrote:

> I see no gleam alluring
> No chance of splendid booty or of gain
> If I endure, I must go on enduring
> And my reward for bearing pain is pain
> Yet, though the thrill, the zest, the hope is gone
> Something in me keeps fighting on.

Meanwhile, General Tomoyuki Yamashita headed his army toward Singapore, at the tip of the Malay peninsula and a key stronghold of the British Empire in the Pacific. Yamashita had 26,000 well-trained troops. British Lieutenant General Percival had almost 87,000 troops, but had no tanks; and his fighter planes were obsolete single-seat monoplane Brewster Buffaloes, which were useless against the Japanese, partly because the crews were not well trained and because the British air force did not have the radar (and fighter direction systems), which they had had in the 1940 Battle of Britain.

The people of Malay were terrified of the Japanese tanks and mechanized armies that advanced on the poorly prepared Allied forces. Singapore's citizens were bombarded by Japanese bombers and fighter planes. The two million people that were there soon ran out of food, water, ammunition, and supplies.

On 15 February 1942, Singapore had to surrender its 60,000 troops to the Japanese as well as all of Singapore.

The rapid advance of General Homma's army toward Manila, and Yamashita's fast drive down the Malay peninsula toward Singapore, had led the Japanese high command to pull out one division to send to Java, where on 5 March 1942, the Dutch surrendered 100,000 Dutch, British, and Australian troops and 80,000 civilians to the Japanese — a month earlier than the master plan had dictated. Many of these prisoners died at the ruthless hands of the Japanese; Australians, in particular, were bayoneted to death. In Malaya, nurses were forced to march into the sea as the Japanese gunners fired at them. Only one nurse survived; 5,000 Chinese were beheaded there. Now you can understand the terror that struck the hearts of people the world over.

The Japanese officers also struck, killed, or tortured the men under them all the way down the ranks. They were violent throughout history and were masters in the ways of torture. They were especially cruel to Chinese and Filipinos. I have read that the Japanese would tie the legs together of a pregnant woman about to give birth, which would maximize the pain of both the mother and baby until they both died. Men would be stretched out and staked down over a cut-off bamboo thicket; almost over night the sprouting bamboo shoots would begin to penetrate the helpless victim, resulting in an agonizing death. Apparently the Nazis were equally as vicious. One wonders what prompts the human race to stoop to such savagery.

Back on Bataan, by April 1942 there was some friction and confusion amongst our troops as the big attack came, and commanders disagreed on what to do. Major General Wainwright thought about surrender, but General MacArthur wired, "I am utterly opposed under any circumstances or condition to the ultimate capitulation of this command. If food fails you will initiate an attack upon the enemy." President Roosevelt even gave orders forbidding surrender. But General Wainwright could not muster enough men for even a feeble counterattack. Our men were being bombed and shelled mercilessly. Defying orders not to surrender from General Wainwright, Major General Edward King decided they could go on no longer. Some of his men had not eaten in three days. On 9 April 1942 he carried a flag of truce to a Japanese commander. As the U.S. flag passed by, most of the firing on Bataan stopped.

General Nakayama was disappointed that it was Major General King instead of Major General Wainwright who had surrendered, but Wainwright was by that time over on Corregidor fighting the Japanese. Major

General King was questioned at length. Men were huddled in bunches, some were weeping, partly in relief that it was over, partly from defeat, and partly from exhaustion.

Major General King's surrender of 76,000 men was the biggest defeat the United States had ever suffered; 12,000 of these men were our American boys. They were rounded up and started on the infamous Bataan Death March.

Japanese General Homma insisted that all forces on the Philippines surrender. It took several days for all of the U.S. commanders throughout the islands to capitulate, as many were opposed. But in view of the fact that General Wainwright's troops were being held hostage and probably would all be slaughtered, our generals finally surrendered one by one. Some men, however, fled to the hills to join guerilla forces, which harassed the Japanese throughout the rest of the war.

Ironically, General Homma was relieved of his command because he didn't overthrow the Philippines fast enough to suit the Imperial command and because he was too lenient on the Filipinos and the Americans. After the war he was tried by the Allies as a war criminal, convicted, and executed.

The troops who surrendered on Bataan were forced to march 65 miles north to Camp O'Donnell, a former U.S. barracks near Clark Field air base used to house prisoners of war. About 70,000 troops, 12,000 of whom were American soldiers, and 26,000 civilians began this march. They would receive no rations, almost no water, and it was very hot. The Japanese showed their sadistic nature and disdain for the prisoners. Some were forced to remove their clothes and stand in the blistering sun surrounded by the dead and bloated bodies of their comrades. The wounded were kicked awake and forced to march. Some prisoners were beaten with wrenches, gun butts, clubs, and swords, and some were bayoneted as they tried to drink from the irrigation ditches. A very few Japanese expressed and showed a little sympathy.

The Japanese didn't have the planning facilities or the transportation to undertake such an operation. Japanese soldiers repeatedly shot, bayoneted, or beheaded prisoners. One prisoner was counting the headless corpses by the roadside until he reached 27; then he decided he had better not continue, so he just stared straight ahead as he walked. The prisoners would get so tired they would sit or fall down. Those too weak to get up were shot. When a group of Filipinos saw an artesian well and rushed to get a drink, Japanese guards shot all six. The atrocities mounted.

Some prisoners managed to fall out of line and escape. Some groups of prisoners were not tortured very much. And not all of the prisoners had to march. Some of the injured, and others chosen seemingly by chancc, got to ride in trucks.

The last mile of the march passed the small town of San Fernando. There crowds of people lined the roadside trying to give assistance to the weary soldiers. The guards let up on their punishment, but some of the prisoners just fell over dead; others received some rice. Some of the prisoners were loaded directly into closed railroad cars and shipped out with no food or water, very little air — sick, vomiting, and dying.

Finally, they began getting some food. But more died on the Bataan Death March than on the battlefields of Bataan. A Colonel Dyess, writing of his POW experience there, stated that he marched 85 miles in six days on one mess kit of rice. The marching columns for some reason would be made to double back down the road at night, and hence the different mileage of some of the different groups. Between 7,000 and 10,000 of the Filipino and U.S. soldiers died from thirst and hunger.

At Camp O'Donnell, the destination, prisoners died at first at the rate of 20 American soldiers and 150 Filipino soldiers per day. This soon increased to 50 Americans and 500 Filipinos per day. No treatment, no medication — no nothing. The men stood in line six to ten hours for a sip of water at the one water hydrant.

The men were told that they were captives, not prisoners of war, and as such would be held without rights or privileges. Soon the prisoners could not find enough able-bodied men to bury their dead, as they had all been reduced to skin and bones. Of the march survivors, 40 percent died as a result of torture and malnutrition.

Meanwhile, General Wainwright was still holding out in Corregidor under constant and ferocious shelling and bombing day and night. Wainwright wrote President Roosevelt:

> . . . there is a limit of human endurance, and that limit has long since passed. Without prospect of relief, I feel it my duty to my country and my gallant troops to end this useless effusion of blood and human sacrifice.

The thousand-bed hospital at Malinta Tunnel on Corregidor was quickly filling up with the sick and dying. On 6 May 1942, General Wainwright sent this message to President Roosevelt:

> With broken heart and head bowed in sadness but not in shame I report to your excellency that today I must arrange terms for the surrender of the fortified island of Manila Bay.

On that day, Lieutenant General Wainwright surrendered to the Japanese on Corregidor. At the time, General MacArthur violently condemned General Wainwright for the surrender and thought the men should have fought to the death — though he later regretted that statement.

The Japanese military held all prisoners in contempt and were bolstered by a fanatical belief in divine guidance and spiritual and military supremacy, as well as their planned domination of the Far East and eventually the world. They were anxious to build a vast war machine. The height of their fanaticism was evidenced later by the kamikaze — "divine wind" — attacks on U.S. ships. Emperor Hirohito of Japan was seen by all Japanese, including the generals and admirals, as god. And these men were willing to risk all, sacrificing their lives to accomplish their purpose.

After the Philippines surrendered, many American and Filipino soldiers and civilians who had escaped formed guerrilla groups. They fed and cared for other escapees who were starved and diseased. There were many men and women who performed dangerous and heroic deeds for the poor people throughout the islands, including getting aid into the prison camps. The guerrillas formed intricate spy and sabotage networks. The people there were all expecting General MacArthur to keep his promise to return.

Many of the men on Bataan were my classmates and friends. Can you imagine the impact on Deming and other small towns in America that had so many young men removed from them? Of the 87 or so who went to the Philippines from the Deming area, 36 died; 51 others returned home in poor health, a result of the Death March and constant torture and starvation while incarcerated.

Some of them were sent to Japan to work in factories and mines. Sergeant Ike Garrett, one of my friends who went to the Philippines from Deming and was a prisoner of war, wrote that the American losses had been pretty light up until the Death March; but when they started running out of food and supplies, and then the surrender and the subsequent march, the death toll really began to mount up. He was sent to work in a Japanese leather factory. He recalled that the men stole leather at night to be boiled and eaten — far better than their meager rations.

Lieutenant Lee, author of the poems quoted, died on a Japanese freighter headed for Japan which was sunk by American planes. The prisoners had been kept below deck in these ships in such wretched conditions that no doubt death was viewed as a relief. The prisoners who did survive were shipped to Japan and Manchuria, and other areas, to work in factories and mines. James Donaldson, who had been a 4-H leader in Deming, was badly wounded on a sinking ship but was rescued by another, and I heard that he was even put on a third ship and taken to a prison camp. All these men suffered from ill health throughout the remainder of their lives.

Lee Pelayo, a former POW, wrote, "We can tell you all this stuff but you will never understand unless you have been there."

People in our country tried to blame our leaders from President Roosevelt down through the admirals and generals, but in reality our whole country was to blame for not maintaining our preparedness.

As I write this book, my mind keeps going back to the men, women, and children in the Philippines, to the National Guard units from New Mexico, and to my home town and my friends.

Luna County, New Mexico, where Deming is the county seat, had about the highest percentage loss of any U.S. community. Out of 1,841 men from New Mexico, 810 died from starvation and brutality inflicted by the Japanese.

In Deming, New Mexico, there is a fine museum in the old National Guard Armory. Beside it is a beautiful monument erected in memory of those who served their country on Bataan and Corregidor. The monument depicts a ragged and emaciated soldier trying to support an even more ragged and sick soldier. At its dedication, the roll was called as it had been in prison camps, and the surviving veterans answered in Japanese as had been required of them. Some were unable to stand. This was a very moving ceremony.

Since that time, most of these men are gone. One of the survivors told me that he did not like the idea of killing people but that he wouldn't be here today, nor would hundreds of thousands of others of our military be here, had we not ended the war with the atomic bomb.

After the war I became involved with making a living, and I put it all behind me. I moved to Arizona, and didn't often see my friends that had been involved in the Philippine ordeal. When we did meet, I surely didn't think they wanted to discuss that traumatic part of their lives. But now most of these men are gone, and we haven't told our children and grandchildren very much about it.

Chapter 4

Induction and Training

IN APRIL 1942 when I was accepted into the U.S. Army Air Corps, I became a private unassigned, for $21.00 a month. In August, I received orders to report to basic training in Nashville, Tennessee, and was accepted as an aviation cadet. I went to Preflight Training at Maxwell Field, Alabama, on 12 September 1942. I attended Primary Flying School at Embry Riddle School of Flying in Arcadia, Florida, from 20 November 1942 through January 1943, flying a Stearman Kaydet PT-17 biplane with a 220 hp Continental radial engine, and then went on to Basic Flying School, 31 January, at Bainbridge Army Airfield, Montgomery, Alabama, in the low-wing, fixed undercarriage Vultee BT-13, with a 450 hp Pratt and Whitney engine known as the Vibrator. In Advanced Flying School, in Marianna, Florida, I was in the North American AT-6 Texan, with the 600 hp Pratt and Whitney engine. I received my wings and second lieutenant rank on 28 May 1943. After a ten-day leave, which I spent visiting my girlfriend and my folks, I reported to Key Field to the 48th Bomber Group in Meridian, Mississippi, on 9 June 1943, then on to Harding Field, to the 85th Bomber Group, 305th Squadron, on 14 June 1943.

When I was in Preflight School, a bunch of boys came to our class of 43E who were uncooperative and disrespectful, and worst of all, unpatriotic. They had no intention of wanting to defend our country, wouldn't obey orders — nothing. Thus, 55 percent of our class was washed out immediately and was sent to the Infantry, and I don't know where else. The reason for the "wash-out" was their attitude. At the time, I wondered "what kind of deal is this?" It wasn't until later that I would realize just how important attitude is. Most of the remainder of our class was from Texas — they were "gung-ho" — quite a contrast to the wash-outs. I was from New Mexico, which the Texans called "just a small part of Texas."

One fellow in our class wanted to fly so badly in Primary Flying School — and he was good, too — but he got air sick every time he went up. The instructor was determined to stay with the boy for as long as it took, and though the poor guy kept trying, he had to wash the plane out after every flight. I don't know what ever happened to him, but both he and that instructor must have had a very good attitude!

On 20 August 1943, I went to a Replacement Training Unit, 499th Squadron, in Baton Rouge, Louisiana, and flew the A-36 Apache, the dive-bomber version of the P-51. Actually, it was a P-51 Mustang with dive brakes and single-stage supercharger. It was used in Africa. Built by North American, it was powered with an Allison V-1710-87 engine, whereas the later P-51s were powered with a British Rolls-Royce Merlin, and then with the 1,300 hp Packard-built V-1650-3, which offered an improvement in performance. The last production model was the P-51H, a lightweight version that was intended primarily for use in the Pacific, with a 2,218 hp V-1650-9 engine. The P-51 Mustang was probably the best fighter airplane built during World War II. To a farm kid who had

The author's Pilot Log Book begins with an entry on 25 November 1942, with a 35-minute training flight in a PT-17 Stearman with a Continental 220 hp engine at Carlstrom Field, Arcadia, Florida. The first flight, he notes, was "straight and level." The next day he "learned to taxi the plane."

more hours behind a team of horses than in a car, the P-51 had tremendous horsepower and torque.

While in cadet training, a flight of P-47 Thunderbolts came roaring in to give us a pep talk. We were wide-eyed and bushy-tailed and listened intently. We asked questions about requirements and qualifications to be a bomber pilot, navigator, bombardier, transport pilot, etc. One of our group asked what it would take to be a fighter pilot, and the P-47 pilots responded with: "Can you count to 10?" I knew I was in!

We practiced follow-through landings (touch and go) in A-36s, but there were so many things involved in this exercise that I have now forgotten the sequence. I do recall that when landing, you had to change your fuel selector valve to reserve tank, lower the landing gear, lower the landing flaps, advance the mixture control to full rich, advance the prop control to high rpm, change the oil-cooler flaps, slow the air speed to 110 mph, control the rudder, change the trim tabs, flare out the glide at 110 mph, and then touch down. But when you touched down, you couldn't see anything directly ahead of you because the nose of the plane was up in the air. All of this was done above 100 mph — full throttle, almost full rudder, with

DATE 19 42	AIRCRAFT IDENT. MARK	MAKE - MODEL AND HORSEPOWER OF AIRCRAFT	FROM	TO	CLASS OR TYPE			DURATION OF FLIGHT Total Time to Date
					2-Se-L O-P-B			0:00
11/25/42	U.S. Army	PT-17 Stearman Continental-220	LOCAL Carlstrom Field, Arcadia, Fla.		✓			0:35
11/26/42	"	"	"	"	✓			1:20
11/27/42	"	"	"	"	✓			2:05
11/28/42	"	"	"	"	✓			2:55
11/30/42	"	"	"	"	✓			3:40
12/1/42	"	"	"	"	✓			4:35
12/2/42	"	"	"	"	✓			5:20
12/4/42	"	"	"	"	✓			6:20
12/5/42	"	"	"	"	✓			7:20
12/7/42	"	"	"	"	✓			8:00
12/8/42	"	"	"	"	✓			8:50
12/9/42	"	"	"	"	✓			10:05
12/10/42	"	"	"	"	✓			11:04
12/12/42	"	"	"	"	✓			11:44
CARRY TOTALS FORWARD TO TOP OF NEXT PAGE								11:44

SOLO FLIGHT TIME			LINK	DUAL INSTRUCTION as Instructor or Student			REMARKS: Each maneuver and the time spent thereon, attested to by the Instructor is to be entered in this column for all instruction received. Any serious damage to the aircraft MUST be entered here also.
Day	Night	Instrument		Day	Night	Instrument	
0:00			0:00	0:00			
				0:35			First flight - Straight and level
				0:45			Learned to taxi the plane
				0:45			He showed me stalls and spins and gliding turns
				0:50			Same as yesterday and climbing turns
				0:45			Made many mistakes - no coordination
				0:55			"S" turns cross-wind
				0:45			Used ailerons in spin - Practice forced landing
				1:00			Practiced throttle coordination - shot landings
				1:00			Shot landings (Drew 100 traffic patterns)
				0:40			Same as before - Landings + take offs
				0:50			Landings + Takeoffs - slight improvement
				1:15			Throttle coordination improving
0:20				0:39			Whoopee!!! Four solo landings (s.w. field) Very happy
0:20				0:20			Four more solo landings " "
0:40				11:04			PILOT'S SIGNATURE William M. [illegible]

Certified By [illegible] #C24143 - Carlstrom Field - 1-18-43

Opposite and above: Facing-page entries from the author's Pilot Log Book.

planes ahead of you, planes behind you. On one occasion, I cut the throttle but didn't let off on the rudder quickly enough, then went full throttle, but got out of sequence. What followed was sort of a blur and created much dust. The tower was highly disgusted, and I was told to taxi back to the parking area, which was awfully close by. My instructor was right there and jumped up on the wing. I was terrified, totally wet with sweat. It was miserably hot in Baton Rouge, and they hadn't even thought of air coolers in that airplane!

I just knew that this was the end of my flying career. The instructor asked if I was scared, and I said, "Yes, Sir."

He calmly told me, "You know, Gaskill, I have been flying for a long time, but I was never able to land on the flight line [*parking area*]. Maybe you had better quit for the day."

In Baton Rouge we would take off many times right over giant oil tanks. The other takeoff direction was over downtown Baton Rouge. We always thought that if the engine ever conked out, my, what a mess! It was very stressful trying to gear up to that kind of necessary horsepower.

The flight schools used comics or cartoons as visual aids to teach us to fly, which were quite effective. And we had neat little sayings like the "commandments for flying." One such commandment was,

> My son, hearken unto thy teaching and forsake not the laws of prudence for the reckless shall not inhabit the earth for long.

Another was

> More praiseworthy is he that toucheth down softly than he who loopeth and rolleth till some damsel stares in amazement at his daring.

Our flight check list was reinforced with the mnemonic "All Good Pilots Must Land Fine Check." The first letter of each word stood for something to check: A (altimeter), G (gas), P (prop pitch), M (mixture control), L (landing gear), F (flaps), C (carburetor and heat controls).

We have all heard accounts of "I learned about flying from that . . ." — hair-raising predicaments and dumb stunts that make interesting reading — as well as "stories and tales":

> Two old veteran fliers met at a reunion. One had become a "bird colonel," while the other was still a second lieutenant. The colonel asked the second lieutenant, "Why, after all those years of flying, were you never promoted?"
>
> The second lieutenant said, "Well, one time we were standing scramble alert in the islands [that is where you sit under or near your plane until the klaxon sounds and we all rush to our planes and take off after some "bogey"]. We had this little monkey as a mascot and he would shinny down the tree, jump in the plane with me, and away we would go. One day I had this really good poker hand, and wouldn't you know the klaxon sounded. I didn't much want to right then, but that crazy little monkey scurried down that tree, jumped in the plane, and took off without me. He even shot down a Zero, no less. When he got back, I was going to take that goofy little dude up and kick his little seat out over the jungle somewhere, but no, the Army brass found out about it and busted me and promoted him to colonel, and he was made the CO. That's why I am still a second lieutenant!"

Or what about the tale of the country kid who joined the paratroopers. On his first flight up, the sergeant told him, "Don't worry a bit; you jump. Count to ten, and pull the rip cord. If nothing happens, you have another parachute. Count to ten and pull the other rip cord. Your chute will open, and you will float right down to where a truck will be waiting for you."

The country boy did as he was told. He counted to ten, pulled his rip cord, and nothing happened. He counted to ten again and pulled the other rip cord, and still nothing happened. Greatly agitated, he looked down at the ground and said, "Those lying dudes. I'll bet that lousy truck doesn't even show up."

The military and wartime offer many amusing tales amidst the gravity. One of my friends told me that when he was a prisoner of war in Japan being transported back and forth to work in the mines, little Japanese children standing by the roadside would put their fingers under their lower eyelids and pull down. He wondered about that until he remembered that when he was a little kid and passed some Japanese Americans, he would put his fingers at the edges of his eyes and stretch them sideways as far as they would go. "What goes around comes around."

William M. Gaskill and Elvena Ford, 4 July 1943.

After I had received my wings, I asked Elvena Ford to marry me. We had been going together for a long time and were engaged. In those days you had to get permission from the Commanding Officer to get married because some girls would marry guys going overseas just so they would get the insurance if anything happened to him, and the military frowned on that.

The Commanding Officer did, however, give us permission, providing. . . . Now there is the right way, the wrong way, and the Army way to do everything, and we had to do it the Army way. They didn't want to interrupt the flight training, but if I would agree to take all of my overseas immunization shots, I would be grounded for a couple of days during which time I could get married. What kind of sick deal was this? I must have been desperate!

I called Elvena — I believe it was my first long distance telephone call! She was in Kingman, Arizona, working for the Army Ordnance Depot.

The plan was for her to pick up her mother in Deming, New Mexico, and proceed to Baton Rouge. In the meantime, I was sent to Barksdale Field near Shreveport, Louisiana, for high-altitude testing and training where we learned the necessity of using our oxygen masks (and the consequences if we didn't — I passed out!).

Elvena and her mother arrived in Baton Rouge, but no one was there to meet them. Elvena had sent me a telegram which said she would arrive on Saturday, 31 June 1943. She insists to this day that this is not what she sent. Somehow that date didn't seem to coincide with anything! Anyway, upon arrival, she called the base and asked where she could locate "Second Lieutenant William M. Gaskill."

They couldn't tell her that, of course. "There is a war on, you know."

"Will he be back?" she asked.

"Oh, yes, he'll be back," she was told.

"When?" she probed.

"We can't tell you that," they replied.

I returned in a couple of days to find a message to call the King Hotel, which I did. I was told that Mrs. Ford and her daughter had left that morning. But I was to discover that there are more Fords out there than one might ever imagine. The base, in typical GI fashion, had mixed her message with somebody else's. When I had the presence of mind enough to go and pick up my mail, my bride-to-be had written me a letter via my company headquarters. I finally found the right Ford! And we proceeded with our plans to marry.

The next day was the 4th of July. The Commanding Officer walked her down the aisle, and we had a nice little ceremony and party, even though nobody had any money to spend. Afterward, the honeymoon consisted of going across the Mississippi on a ferry boat — hot and stinky, with mosquitoes everywhere.

I was not allowed to live off the base, but my best man at the wedding, who happened to be red-headed, said that he would sleep in my bed when they had bed check and then run around and jump into his. Well, it didn't take the Army long to figure out there was only one red-headed guy spending nights in the outfit instead of two. Consequently, I was grounded and confined to base for a week. Elvena and I sat in the Officers Club all day every day. This was not too exciting, so we started putting nickels in the slot machine, and she eventually hit the jackpot. Then, in youthful exuberance, and to break the monotony, I ran out the back door to dive into the swimming pool. However, I had neglected to notice that there was not much water in the pool; and consequently, my forehead, nose, and chin lost considerable hide. I was kidded for a long time about my newly acquired battle scars.

On 20 August 1943, 12 of us from the Replacement Unit were transferred to Waycross, Georgia, where we were to check out in the P-39 Airacobra. The P-39 had an Allison V-1710 engine but only a single-stage supercharger. Maximum speed was about 330 mph at 5,000 feet. However, you could dive this plane to 500 mph. The wingspan was 34 feet, length 30 feet 2 inches, height 12 feet 5 inches. It carried only about 100 gallons, and later 120 gallons, of gas, rendering it a very short-range, low-altitude fighter, but it was really not designed as a fighter anyway, but more for ground support. It was a little single-seat, single-engine fighter plane. A month later we went to Harris Neck, Georgia, where we practiced aerial gunnery over the Atlantic Ocean with a bomber pulling the tow target. I would not have wanted to be that bomber crew with a bunch of trigger-happy new pilots shooting at their target. I went "under the hood" — instrument flying — to solo off a short field, which was scary.

Although the P-39 had a very poor aerial combat record, it was excellent in the jungles of the South Pacific, dive bombing, skip bombing, and strafing boats, guns, bivouac areas, and supply dumps. This plane's engine was behind the pilot with the drive shaft underneath going forward between the pilot's legs to a gearbox in the nose. The hollow shaft carried the propeller and a 37mm cannon, its barrel firing right through the hollow propeller shaft, plus four .50-caliber machine-guns and a 500-pound bomb.

I am convinced that most pilots with very few flying hours in this plane were terrified to use it to its fullest potential — the flight characteristics were really weird. The engine behind you gave it, as the cowboys would say, a sun-fishing feeling, trying to slip sideways out from under you. If you stalled, you might slip into a tumble — a maneuver like no other plane. The pilots who had that happen could never fully explain what went on (and neither could Bell). If they went into a flat spin, they could hardly get the nose down to recover. In other planes you could kick off into a spin, put the nose down, and then recover; but there was never any reason to stall except touching down on landing on a short strip. Lieutenant Ben Jones, later one of the pilots in our 68th Squadron, once had to bail out of a flat spin at a low altitude and dead engine — a very narrow escape. His chute caught in a tree.

But the P-39 was the quickest plane off the ground. You could get in it fast, revving up while taxiing toward the strip, dragging your brakes, holding back while taxiing — all the while checking the mag, instruments, putting down flaps, etc. Sometimes we didn't even stop at the runway, already being part way up to speed. When we were standing scramble alert, the engine had already been warmed up and hopefully it would stay warm enough. This wasn't exactly safe, but we gave it full throttle and went barreling down the runway. If the runway was wide enough, we took off in formation.

We sank many barges and boats and inflicted much damage to the enemy. The tricycle gear was a great advantage. The P-39 had good visibility, whereas with conventional planes, it was a little slower and riskier trying to get a lot of planes in the air or landing in a short time.

After I had about 240 hours of combat time in a P-39, the planes were taken to Russia where they really used the aircraft right — for knocking out heavy artillery, strafing troops, tanks, and supply lines. The Russians loved it!

At Waycross, there was a P-47 Thunderbolt, and I asked our Captain Harding if he would check me out in it. He agreed, but told me to go to lunch first while he made sure it would fly okay. The captain took off in it, it crashed, and he was killed. I couldn't find out any details, but I surely felt bad.

The Bell Company came out with a synchronized propeller and throttle control arrangement for the P-39, but they had set the rpm too low. We said it was too slow, but they didn't believe us. To prove the point, I started off down the runway at their specifications on manifold pressure. I held the aircraft on the ground until the last moment, then really gunned it and just cleared the end of the runway. Everybody was sweating it out. The manufacturer's setting of 30 inches of mercury would not cut it on low rpm. On the flight line the next day, a large poster of a P-39 appeared, showing me carrying the plane on my back as fast as I could with my tongue hanging out, and labeled "30-inch Gaskill."

I recall an error I made one day when I got into a plane with very large lettering "V-10" — no numbers on the inside of the plane. I thought I had gotten into plane number V-12. Later, when I asked the tower for landing clearance for V-12, the tower paused and said, "We don't see you V-12, where are you?"

"I'm on approach," I replied.

They screamed for me to "Pull up and go around." I did, but saw no V-12 anywhere. What a mix-up; I was very embarrassed.

The P-39 had weird flight characteristics, and for the first few hours in this plane you would have to be as careful as a naked man in a cactus patch with a loose rattlesnake!

I was transferred from Georgia to Tallahassee, Florida, to await overseas shipment. Our orders read "Destination FJ736." Our group comic, Lieutenant Bruce B. Grooms, said, "Boys, we're going to the Fijis." Would you believe, he was right!

Elvena was with me until I left Tallahassee, then she and another wife, with a baby, drove back to Deming. They had a rough trip in an old car as I went by slow train to San Francisco.

In California we boarded a plane for Hawaii. By then, I really wasn't in the mood to go. I was already homesick. The night was dark and stormy; lightning lit up the aircraft, and you could see the skin on the wings wrinkle. It looked like the rivets would pop out. Some guys in the front of the plane were noisy and having a good time, and I just wished they would let me sleep. Among them was someone named *John Wayne* and his group, on the way to entertain troops overseas. Who was John Wayne?!

We reached Hawaii, refueled, and the plane was sprayed down with DDT. We immediately loaded up, and headed out. So much for Hawaii! I'll never go back there. We finally did catch up with our outfit in the Fiji Islands where they were training for another combat tour at the front.

Chapter 5

Duty Calls — The 13th Air Force

THE 13TH AIR FORCE was created in January 1943 in the South Pacific, with General George C. Kenney as head, and was made up of some U.S. Army Air Forces units that were already operating in that area: the Heavy Bombardment groups of the 5th, 11th, 307th, and 868th "Snooper" Squadrons, the Medium Bombardment groups of the 69th and 70th Bomb Squadrons, 13th Troop Carrier Group, and a night fighter squadron, plus the 347th Fighter Group, and the 18th Fighter Group.

①

Date	Type of Machine	Number of Machine	Duration of Flight	Character of Flight	Pilot

Buttons - New Hebrides 1 Jan 1944
New Caledonia 4 Jan 1944
Nandi Fiji 5 Jan 1944
— 68th Ftr Sqdn. —
Time - 435 hrs - (203 hrs Ftr)
Col. Willard C.O.
Reported in - 6 Jan 1944
Flew one hour 7 Jan 1944
P-39 D-1 orientation
Flew one hour - 8th Jan
Formation with - element lead
Very rusty on flying these boys
are good fliers and know their
stuff. It is very pretty here
warm but not to warm nor
too many mosquitos. Natives
are very black friendly and
polite They don't speak English
Their hair is bushy and black. They
grow pineapple sugar cane + rice

Total time to date,

16—18616

The author's Aviators Flight Log Book entry for 6 January 1944 notes: "Reported in." The 7 January entry notes: "Flew one hour" and "P-39 D-1 orientation."

(2)

PASSENGERS	REMARKS

The town is small - all of the
buildings are lined on one
side of the street. I bought
my darling wife a souvenir -
The mountains are beautiful
- about 4000 ft I guess. We
fly only about one hour per day.
Guess I'll write Elvera - Bye now!
9 Jan 1944 Sunday and it
has been a beautiful day - however
a hurricane is on the way +
we are on the alert for it. Bruce
got a good sun burn. Have
written several letters. Puzzling letter from Elvera
10 Jan 1944 Today we received a
good briefing lecture also some
excellent news. The planes are
grounded. So I guess we won't
fly anymore from here. Will go
to the show presently. The hurricane
never reached us but did have
a slight wind + rain. Cloudy all morn

16—18616 GPO

Date	Type of Machine	Number of Machine	Duration of Flight	Character of Flight	Pilot

Buttons - New Hebrides 1 Jan 1944
New Caledonia 4 Jan 1944
Nandi Fiji 5 Jan 1944 —
— 68th Ftr Sqdn.
Time - 435 hrs - (203 hrs Ftr)
Col. Milliof C.O.
Reported in - 6 Jan 1944
Flew one hour 7 Jan 1944
P-39 D-1 orientation
Flew one hour - 8th Jan
Formation with - element lead
Very rusty on flying these boys
are good fliers and know their
stuff. It is very pretty here
warm but not to warm nor
too many mosquitos. Natives
are very black friendly and
polite They don't speak English
Their hair is bushy and black. They
grow pineapple sugar cane + rice

Total time to date,

16—18616

(4)

PASSENGERS REMARKS

13 Jan 1944 I attended a band concert this morning - We moved down to A.T.C. Nothing to do here either. Guess what, a mattress & sheets!! The chow is awful. Quite stormy outside - no dust of course - just rain. Spent some time with the ...

14 Jan 1944. Quite an uneventful day. Have been reading an Ellery Queen mystery, attended a show at the airdrome theater and got soaking wet. Some of the boys went out this morning.

15 Jan 1944 Left Nandi 5 hrs later - P D G + 45 min later - New Cal. (No - Tontouta). Have moved here - I wonder how many more times I will come into this place - Think I will go to Noumea - Numea is a large town for this part of the world but terribly full of soldiers & sailors (It was dirty & nothing but a fight there)

16-18616 GPO

The 347th Fighter Group was composed of the 67th, 68th, 70th, and 339th Fighter Squadrons. These squadrons were transferred around between groups, and bomb loads and ammunitions were changed around to suit the needs of the time. Personnel routinely changed as well.

The primary mission of all American aircraft in the South Pacific was to stop the "Tokyo Express" — the Japanese fast destroyers — from supplying its troops in the Guadalcanal and New Guinea campaigns. Later, the 13th Air Force would support the 5th Air Force along with the Sixth Army as it worked itself through the Solomon Islands.

I joined the 68th Fighter Squadron of the 347th Fighter Group of the 13th Air Force on 7 January 1944. Early on in the 13th I got in on some good aerial combat, but the 5th Air Force did most of it and racked up an impressive kill record. Their aerial feats were the more spectacular, but our part in knocking out ground installations, shipping, and supply bases was invaluable, too.

The 13th Air Force came under the jurisdiction of COMAIRSOLS — Commander of Air Operations of the Solomons — under U.S. Army General Nathan G. Twining, with the Navy, Marine, Army, and New Zealand Air Groups all operating there. A naval officer was later put in charge of coordinating all air forces activities in the area of the South to Southwest Pacific. The 13th, or "Jungle Air Force," had set up headquarters on Espiritu Santo, New Hebrides, near the Fiji Islands. The 13th later moved to the Solomon Islands and on up the island chain, through New Britain, New Guinea, Halmahera [*in the Netherlands Indies, north of Ceram*], the Philippines; and it finally flew missions over Okinawa and the other Ryukyu Islands of Japan. We provided ground, sea, and air support, and assault missions for many invasions and landings.

There were about 9,700 men in the 13th Air Force, and about 25 percent of these were service personnel who took care of maintaining our planes. There were Headquarters Company, Quartermaster Company, Signal Company, Engineering Company, Security Company, Fighter Command, and on and on. In addition to the fighter and bomber groups, we had a troop carrier squadron carrying troops and supplies in and out. And the Navy provided an Air Rescue Squadron using amphibious PBY Catalina planes (code name "Dumbo"). Later we acquired our own PBYs, code-named "Playmate." How well I remember Playmate 22. Also, there were the "Photo-Joes," the Lockheed P-38 Lightnings, armed only with a camera, taking pictures of enemy installations. This was certainly a necessary

William M. Gaskill — a photo sent to his wife.

part of the operation of the war. And there was also the Air Evacuation Squadron that flew the wounded out.

On Guadalcanal there were U.S. Navy Grumman F4F Wildcats, P-39 Airacobras (and P-400s, the British version of the P-39), Curtiss P-40 Warhawks/Kittyhawks, and P-38 Lightnings. For a while we were under U.S. Navy Vice Admiral William F. "Bull" Halsey's and later under General MacArthur's command. We did much dive bombing and strafing for them. The P-39s and 400s, made a very poor showing against the Japanese Zeroes, but did excellent work in dive bombing and strafing ground installations in the jungle.

In April 1943, four 13th Air Force P-38s shot down 11 Zeroes. On 12 April our aircraft shot down 77 Japanese planes; we lost only 1. Lieutenant

Marry Shubin shot down six Japanese planes in 45 minutes. Many flying aces were made at about that time and again later, in October 1944, in the invasion of the Philippines. On 18 April 1943, the 339th Fighter Squadron shot down Admiral Yamamoto. During the war, the 475th Fighter Group of the 5th Air Force shot down 551 Japanese aircraft, with a loss of only 56 P-38s — almost a 10-to-1 kill ratio.

The 13th Air Force performed miracles, too, such as our Colonel Leonard Shapiro leading our squadron 1,900 miles round trip to Balikpapan, Borneo, to bomb and strafe oil installations there. Later, the missions were as long as 2,100 miles in a P-38. The 868th Snooper Bomb Squadron flew its B-24s 2,600 miles, followed by a mission of over 3,000 miles, in 18 hours and 40 minutes, to Java.

The 13th Air Force was an assault force when landings were made on Borneo. Our heroes were many, and one in our group was Colonel Robert B. Westbrook, Jr., who knocked down 20 planes before being shot down and killed by a Japanese gunboat. Really, I guess, all the men I flew with were my heroes.

During the war, the 13th Air Force destroyed almost 1,500 planes, sank — and probably sank and damaged — 1.3 million tons of shipping, and bombed and strafed untold thousands of Japanese soldiers. We lost about 500 of our planes.

Early in the war, Marine air groups at Henderson Field on Guadalcanal were flying F4F Wildcats and were doing a great deal of the work before the Army could get enough planes. Most of the aircraft at that time were being sent to the European area. The Marines downed over 800 planes in the Guadalcanal area. Later, the Marines got the Corsair (F4U), the TBF Avenger, and the SBD Dauntless.

We finally figured out that the P-39 Airacobra was an excellent ground support plane, even if it wasn't much good for fighting the Zeroes. You could dive on a target at about 300 or 400 mph. Then, the 339th Squadron got P-38 Lightnings and things began looking up.

In addition, at this time, bombers carried out many missions against Japanese targets. Boeing's B-17 Flying Fortress was replaced by the Consolidated B-24 Liberator because of the extremely long missions. The Martin B-26 Marauder was replaced by the North American B-25 Mitchell, also a very dependable plane. Some of these carried 75mm cannon, certain death to any enemy ship.

Sometimes our bombers were so severely attacked by enemy fighters

A flight of P-39s over New Guinea in 1943.

that our fighter planes were called in to escort them over the target. The P-38 starred in this role. It was extremely long ranging, and the newer Japanese pilots were deathly afraid of the "fork-tailed devil." Also, we had a spare engine in case we lost one!

As the 13th Air Force moved "up the ladder" toward Japan, we flew missions from the Solomon Islands and the Netherlands Indies up to Lingayen in the Philippines, west to Borneo, and southwest to the Celebes Sea. This small air force traveled long distances over the oceans and seas. Later in the war, my buddies even flew across the South China Sea from the Philippines, clear to Saigon in Vietnam to attack Japanese facilities there. Japan needed rubber, tin, quinine, tungsten, and oil; so it had quickly overrun these countries and islands of Southeast Asia and the Southwest Pacific. The Rising Sun seemed unstoppable.

Prior to the formation of the 13th Air Force in 1943, the U.S. Army Air Forces 347th Fighter Group and 339th Fighter Squadron were operating, after having been formed in New Caledonia and then moved to Guadalcanal.

A flight of P-38s — a "deadly force."

On 13 September 1942, a flight of three Airacobras strafed "Bloody Ridge," on Guadalcanal, killing over 600 Japanese soldiers. At that time there were only five Army Air Forces planes and five pilots on the island. Then came the U.S. 339th, 67th, and 70th Fighter Squadrons, which shared their planes. The 339th Squadron had the most experienced pilots, and they had P-38s. In 1943, they were taken into the newly formed 13th Air Force. Back in October 1942, the 67th Squadron on Guadalcanal had had to siphon gas out of abandoned battle-demolished B-17s to make a few missions; then they ran completely out of fuel. And U.S. Navy F4Fs were also flying missions out of Guadalcanal, as were Marine SBDs — a pitifully small beginning. In one of the first aerial combats there, they shot down three Zeroes. Before long, P-38s were escorting P-39s on dive-bombing runs. Soon the 18th Fighter Group, which included the 12th, 44th, and 70th Fighter Squadrons, arrived. P-39s struck repeatedly at Japanese supply dumps and fortifications; and the Marine, Navy, and Army air forces engaged in many aerial battles against the Japanese.

In January 1944, I joined the 68th Fighter Squadron of the 347th Fighter Group. By then, they had gotten plenty of planes, and the Japanese were being driven back.

The 68th was a good squadron to be in, although we engaged in very

Captain Chandler P. Worley — Bill Gaskill's instructor, flight leader in combat, mentor, and friend.

little aerial combat. The insignia was a knight in armor, with a shield and his sword, riding on two lightning flashes.

When I joined the squadron, I was flying P-39s. My flight leader was Captain Chandler P. Worley, a music teacher from Ruleville, Mississippi. What a man! I was most fortunate to join his flight. He was very strict about flying rules. After taking off and forming up, he wanted to see every pilot in his proper place. We were easy to count that way: if one didn't make it, it looked like a tooth was knocked out.

We thought we knew how to fly, but we didn't. He took us up in formation, and we weren't to take our eyes off of him. Once when we were upside down in a loop, I fell out of the loop, and I guess the others did, too. When we landed, he was furious. We went back up and did formation loops, rolls, and everything, but never took our eyes off of him.

We would sometimes strafe and bomb in formation. Sometimes I saw him covered up with ricochet tracers, but that was the way he wanted it. He said that if he was ever shot down, it would be from one of us! Wrong. He was shot down by the enemy, but was rescued and brought back. In teasing his other wing man, Harvey L. Harvey, I would say, "Worley was never shot down when I was with him." Harvey had seen lots of action before I got there.

We went back to Guadalcanal and to Russell Island with our P-39s, and we would dive bomb and strafe Japanese installations all around there. Our forces would take a small area and establish a perimeter, bypassing the rest of the island. We would hold only the airfield and/or supply base.

On missions, sometimes many flights would join together to compose the squadron. In air force jargon, a flight of fighter planes in our outfit meant four airplanes, each flown by one pilot, and composed of the flight leader and his wing man and an element leader and his wing man. Many times we would split up into twos rather than stay all together. Each outfit flew in its own little world.

There were several squadrons in a group and several groups in an air force. A large mission might be composed of many planes. If a mission called for four flights (16 planes), the leader would want to see all planes in their places. Captain Worley's flight was Dancer Red 1. His wing man (me, in this case) was Dancer Red 2. The element leader was Dancer Red 3, and his wing man was Dancer Red 4. The other flights were Dancer Blue, Dancer Yellow, etc.

Typically, in the briefing before the mission, we would be assigned to our regular flight; sometimes there were changes. Then the mission leader would brief us as to the general target area, the heading, number of planes, and specific target for each flight, as well as timing and coordination details. The photographs would be there from the Photo-Joes. Each flight was assigned a specific target to skip bomb, dive bomb, fire bomb, or strafe — a ship, a gun position, troops, installations, or whatever. Our task here was not aerial combat. Sometimes each person might have a definite target to work on; for instance, the first flight might have to knock out a gun position, the next to bomb or strafe a suspected ammunition depot, supply depot, bivouac area, or equipment. And that is why order was necessary. If you missed destroying your alloted gun position, your buddy behind you might be shot down while trying to line up on his target. We would be flying so low that the concussion from our own bombs would jolt us pretty good.

After a strike on the enemy, we would form up close so that the leader could see who was missing. Then we might fly a little more loosely going home, always checking that no enemy could slip up on us and that we had no stragglers. If we had ammunition left, we would use it on secondary targets. As we were getting close to home, we would close it up real close, no matter how tired we were, partly for pride in a smart military formation, but also because we were low on fuel and had to land as quickly as possible.

The first flight would come over the runway at maybe 500 feet and peel up as sharply as possible; man by man, they would peel up immediately, but not in as tight a turn, so in the end it was like a fan unfolding. This was necessary to space the planes in the landing pattern so that we didn't hit the slip stream or run over the guy in front of us, but still get down as quickly as possible. We were nearly always low on fuel and very vulnerable to enemy aircraft at this point.

After we got P-38s, the bomber crews, who were being devastated on long missions by the remaining Japanese aircraft, requested air cover over their targets. We would rendezvous over their planes just before they reached their target. They didn't want to be disturbed on a bomb run, and they certainly didn't want to be shot down. The bombers flew so slowly that it wasn't safe or efficient for our planes to stay with them; we couldn't maneuver quickly at such a low speed.

Near the target, we would fly above and maybe slightly behind the bombers and spread out perhaps line abreast; then we would begin a scissoring, weaving pattern, constantly turning, so that we could keep good speed, continually changing position. The Japanese fighter planes would be up there all right; we were always turning in order to see who might be attacking one of our buddies. The Japs would sometimes feint an attack. We would execute a very tight turn toward them, and they would break off, because there was no way that they wanted a head-on attack with a fork-tailed devil.

We weren't allowed to leave the bombers, because that was what the enemy wanted. But what a temptation it was! We would continue weaving until the bombers were safely off the target. By then the Japanese fighters would usually have disappeared.

We would form up again, lean out our mixture control, back off on the throttle, prop pitch, and rpms, and head for home. Sometimes we would encounter a storm, another reason for flight discipline. Sometimes we would close up so tightly that the prop wash from our wing man's plane would dip us toward him. Sometimes we flew so low in a storm that the props made little spray whirlwinds off the ocean water; but at least we had a guide line. We were safer from collision in bad weather if we were close enough to see each other. If we couldn't see at all, then it was every man for himself and go on instruments. Once my buddy was flying low when he suddenly hit one of those freak tsunami waves — a seismic sea wave. What a jolt. It flattened the bottom of his fuselage, but didn't hurt anything else, and he was able to return home.

At first it was very dangerous to dive the P-38 at much over 500 mph, but after installation of the new diving flaps, the maneuverability greatly improved as well as the ability to get out of a dangerous dive. Because we did a lot of ground strafing and glide bombing, we didn't use flaps as much as the fellows in aerial combat. Neither the P-38, P-47, or P-51 ever achieved the speed of sound — 764 mph at sea level.

As a test pilot of our squadron, I could, with permission, check out any plane on that place. I don't remember how much time I spent studying the operating manual for the P-38 — perhaps an hour or so — no formal instruction — no pilot to go up piggy back. And I don't remember any pilot showing me anything about it. Anyway, if there was any, it was very brief because I started and warmed up the engines and took right off. I was familiar with Allison engines. The airstrip was a little bit short for a P-38, with a cliff at each end of the runway, but flying this plane was what I imagine it would be like to drive a Cadillac after driving a motorcycle.

This magnificent airplane was manufactured by the Lockheed Aircraft Corporation and powered by two Allison engines (V-1710-89 and 91, V-1710 meaning cubic-inch piston displacement). One prop rotated one way and one the other. That feature all but eliminated torque characteristics. The British were being pounded by bombers from Germany, and England desperately needed a pursuit plane to attack these vast armadas. It didn't need to be very maneuverable, but it needed lots of firepower.

Kelly Johnson, of Lockheed, came up with this twin-engine, twin-boom configuration. It wasn't designed as a fighter aircraft, but as an intercepter of bombers. It would have heavy firepower concentrated in the nose instead of the converging firepower from the wing guns. The P-38 was quickly designed and built, and then flown in 1939 by Lockheed's Ben

Kelsey to demonstrate it to the Air Corps. He made a wild dash of 2,400 miles. But on approach to landing, one engine ran away and the other choked up; he hit a tree and crashed on a golf course. It had an impressive speed record, but the crash was a bad setback.

Work continued on modification, and the aircraft finally went into production. The British weren't too impressed with the first models. At high altitude the turbos blew up, partly from the lower quality British fuel. Some of the early P-38s in Britain were converted to photographic planes, what we called F-4s and F-5s, Photo Joes. They outperformed everything. Later in New Guinea, a Photo Joe was jumped by Zeroes. One engine was shot out, which the Photo Joe pilot feathered, and he went into a steep dive on single engine. But even on single engine, our pilot ran away from the Zeroes. These Photo Joe planes were completely unarmed and stripped of everything but the cameras and pilot; they performed an outstanding service during the entire war in both theaters by bringing back pictures of everything that moved or that needed to be moved or destroyed.

But the fault of the P-38s lay in what is called flutter — a high-speed vibration — and compressibility. As new planes were designed, many would be plagued by flutter until the manufacturer made modifications to correct.

Compressibility was something else — if not respected, it was deadly and unpredictable. At 30,000 feet, the speed of sound is less than its 764 mph at sea level, so when you push over in a vertical dive, it isn't long before part of the air going over the top of the wing is approaching the speed of sound, creating shock waves (a breaking up of the normal flow of air) making the plane difficult to control and preventing it from achieving its intended speed. For one thing, I thought the P-38's wing was just too thick. Anyway, at about 540 mph a violent hammering effect set up on the tail, and the tail would break off. Prior to this, the elevator control became as rigid as a post. The only thing to do was to use elevator trim and see if the tail would hang on until you reached a lower altitude or denser air (12,000 to 15,000 feet) and hope the plane would recover. Sometimes there was a reversal of controls, where the more you pulled back on them, the more the plane wanted to tuck under. Dive flaps (brakes) were developed and installed, which really helped, and with them you might dive at 520 mph. As a bonus, the dive brakes greatly helped maneuverability.

Lockheed test pilots Ralph Virden and Mike Burcham and others worked hard to master this problem. Even so, I believe many pilots lost their lives due to compressibility. Virden himself was killed when the tail came off of a P-38 he was testing. Yet even with this negative aspect, P-38 pilots shot down more Japanese Zeroes than those in any other plane.

On my last tour of duty we flew mostly P-38Js powered by two Allison engines of 1,425 hp each. The wing span was 52 feet, length 37 feet 10 inches, and weight about 22,000 pounds loaded, with maximum speed of 360 mph IAS at 5,000, 260 mph at 30,000 feet. The rate of climb was about 3,000 feet per minute in emergency. The P-38L had 1,600 hp in each engine and could carry 4,000 pounds of bombs. In acceptance checks of new planes coming to the squadron, I would write an okay if the aircraft went from parked to 30,000 feet in 20 minutes, and I didn't crowd it to do that. I was told that in emergency the plane would go from parked to 5,000 feet in one and a half minutes, and could fly 400 mph in emergencies.

One other negative aspect of the P-38 — it was riskier to get out of because you might hit the horizontal stabilizer. The best way was to jettison the canopy, turn upside down, and fall out. Most of the boys who did bail out, however, made it okay. Lieutenant Fred Roos of our squadron said he got out all right, but that the plane behind him narrowly missed him. Different speeds dictated different ways to bail out.

Our instructions ordinarily were to climb at 35 inches of mercury (HG), 2,800 rpm, at 160 mph. In combat, we were always to stay above 250 mph, not do tight turns with Zeroes, pull away at full speed on a low-angle dive or climb, then make a 180-degree turn and face the enemy head on. We were to watch for vertical dives, but not to exceed 500 mph, and we would cruise mostly at 200 mph. Of course, all the above was subject to change.

On long missions we would cut our mixture control, rpm, and throttle way back to conserve fuel until over the target. Charles Lindbergh taught us how to get much greater range out of the aircraft.

Major Thomas B. "Tommy" McGuire, one of our country's leading aces, gave his pilots three cardinal rules for engaging in aerial combat in the P-38:

1. Never attempt aerial combat at low altitude.
2. Never let your air speed fall below 300 mph.
3. Never keep your wing tanks in a fight.

On his final mission, he violated all three of his own rules when he turned to aid another pilot with a Zero on his tail. The result was a high-speed stall with no altitude to recover, and a flaming crash; and he was dead, not from bullets, but from the unforgiving laws of aerodynamics.

In the South Pacific, one of the first Japanese fighter planes knocked down by a P-38 in late 1942 in New Guinea, according to author/historian Martin Caidin, was by the 5th Air Force. The P-38's bomb missed the target, which was an airstrip, and hit the water instead. A geyser was thrown up, and a Japanese Zero taking off hit that geyser like it was a brick wall. The Japanese pilot went straight down into the ocean. Strange things happen in combat.

The P-38's extremely long range of over 2,000 miles round trip enabled the aircraft to accompany our long-ranging bombers. The search mission for our Colonel Robert B. Westbrook, Jr., was over 11 hours without refueling, a long time in a fighter plane.

The P-38 seemed a bit tricky on one engine at low speed, but as the pilots gained more hours and more confidence, single-engine operation was not bad at all as long as you respected a few cardinal rules. At low speed and low altitude, with one dead engine, you don't go to full power on the good engine. The plane would go out of control, then turn, then roll. So contrary to what you think you should do, you only add just enough power to keep above stalling speed, then gain speed gradually. (This little bit of information is in case you get the urge to fly a P-38 with one engine dead.) Also, be sure you feather the prop on the dead engine, especially when landing — I should have done that once. And if you had good speed, you could do aerobatics with the P-38 on a single engine.

I have long since forgotten the placement of the necessary switches and controls. Sometimes someone would change the position of a switch; that was a disaster, because the procedure you first learned is what you would always do instantly in a tight spot. For example, if the position of the bomb switch was exchanged with the gun switch, you would probably drop your bomb instead of firing your gun!

Instead of a stick, we had a yoke (1/2 wheel) with many buttons and switches on it. The P-38 had dual controls — one for each engine — throttles, propeller controls, and mixture controls. There were 21 instrument dials, 36 switches, 22 levers, 5 cranks, 2 plungers, 6 buttons (on the steering column), and the radio controls. This all might help explain why at training schools there were as many as 12 crashes per day when teaching new pilots to fly this bird; but it didn't take long for a pilot to feel comfortable in it.

Even after we had been flying combat aircraft, there were a lot of transition accidents as we converted to the Lockheed Lightnings.

There were 18 versions of this plane to meet the needs of the times. The plane cost $125,000. You couldn't buy a used one right now for $1,250,000!

On one occasion, Morriss, my wing man, lost both engines at 23,000 feet, a long way from home, and he coasted all the way in. He got along fine until he came too close to an obstruction at the end of the runway. This was a real dead-stick landing. The obstruction was a tent, and he slipped it to the side slightly. But being so low in air speed, he stalled and hit the bank of a large drainage ditch. So close to being a perfect landing, he had socked down full flaps a second too soon. Had he hit the tent, he would have saved the plane but killed the man inside. The plane was demolished, but Morriss was not hurt.

Our squadron once ran out of ethylene glycol (antifreeze) and so our engineering officer sent me to get some. Many of our planes were grounded for lack of sufficient coolant, but we didn't have the clout or priority to obtain it. Our Allison engines were liquid cooled, not air cooled like the radial engines of most of the other planes.

Anyway, Captain Lewis Jarrell, Engineering Officer of our squadron, said, "Get it." My crew chief said he knew how, so we took off in a P-38 with a modified 300-gallon belly tank. He rode piggy back; we had taken out the big radio behind my head, and he was hunkered down across my shoulders with his head right beside mine. He didn't have room for a parachute, so he didn't have one. We took off, and I guess we flew about 200 miles to a supply base (my diary didn't show where this base was — and it was illegal to keep a diary anyway). My sergeant said, "You keep the man at the front desk busy talking; I'll tell you when we're ready."

Well, I don't know how he did it, but he "acquired" enough antifreeze to fill the belly tank. Then he came in and said he was ready to go. All would have been well, but when I arrived on that island, the most awful allergic reaction hit me. The airstrip was a beautiful, long, wide, white runway. Tears were filling my eyes and running down my face; I had to pull off my goggles, which made the blinding white even whiter. I couldn't read my instruments, but I had flown that plane long enough that I thought I could "feel" the aircraft into the air. I think the sergeant was really worried. I could faintly make out the palm trees on either side of the runway.

I managed to get lined up on the runway, though I couldn't see the tower or the green light if they flashed one. I expected the Military Police at any minute, so I shoved both throttles and props forward and away we went. I have no idea what that takeoff must have looked like, but I held as straight a course as I could and automatically pulled up my wheels and flaps and adjusted the other controls. By the time I reached 10,000 feet, my eyes began to clear up. We got home with the antifreeze, and the Squadron could fly again. What a way to fight a war!

Between the lack of supplies and the occasional stealing of clocks and some of our other instruments (altimeters, compasses) at one of our staging places, we seemed to be fighting more than the enemy! You could not lead a flight or fly alone through some of the tropical storms without all of your instruments. Once, upon discovering the missing equipment, we went tearing off to report to the Commanding Officer. In a calm voice, he told us, "Shoot the sons of bitches!" Word got around fast, and there was no more of that problem.

Chapter 6

My Tour Overseas

Departed — Overseas!!
Hickam Field
Canton Island
Nandi, Fiji
P.D.G. New Caledonia 20th Dec 1943
Flew L-4B
Guadalcanal 28 Dec 1943
Buttons & Efate 31 Dec 1943
Happy New Year!!
Buttons — New Hebrides 1 Jan 1944
New Caledonia 4 Jan 1944
Nandi, Fiji 5 Jan 1944
68th Ftr Sqdn.
Reported in 6 Jan 1944
Flew one hour 7 Jan 1944
P-39D-1 Orientation
Flew one hour 8th Jan

Early in 1944 on Ondonga Island, 347th Fighter Group, 13th Air Force, in the Northern Solomons. Top row — Captain Street, Major Leonard R. Shapiro, ?, Captain Stephen J. Sun, Lieutenant Bruce B. Grooms. Bottom row — Lieutenant William M. Gaskill, Captain Antonio M. DeAngelo, Captain Arpod Artwohl, Captain Claude V. McLemore.

AND SO BEGINS the log of my tour in the South Pacific!

My first reaction was that it was very pretty, warm — but not too warm, with far too many mosquitoes. The natives didn't speak English; they grew pineapple, sugar cane, and rice. It was a small town with all of the buildings on one side of the street with beautiful mountains in the background.

I recorded that the fliers all seemed to be good and knew their stuff. Although I felt most fortunate to be in Captain Chandler P. Worley's flight, I wondered why he picked me. Perhaps it was because he saw in me a glimmer of potential as a fighter pilot. Anyway, our missions were many and interesting.

My diary of this first combat tour gives an interesting look into a young pilot at war. But I am somewhat distressed to read now my words stating we had "a lot of fun" when we were killing people and creating destruction everywhere. I know the excitement and thrill was there, but fun? I guess that is part of war. Perhaps I received such satisfaction from the missions because I knew I had friends who were being tortured and killed by the Japanese in the Philippines. I wanted to avenge them all, though I real-

The "Lightning Lancers" — the 68th Fighter Squadron, 347th Fighter Group, 13th Air Force, in 1944.

ize that the Bible says, "Vengeance is mine, I will repay sayeth the Lord."

12 January 1944 — Nice day same as usual. Nothing to do. I went down to buy some ice cream. There was a big fight getting under way. This was between the coloured troops and the white. A paddlefoot [*a sailor*] was there so I didn't do anything. He stopped it. After he left, though, it started in again, so I had to take a hand! I stepped between them. Of course it isn't good to disobey or strike an officer over here as he would be court martialed. . . . I do not like to pull my rank on anyone, but this was one time that I was glad that I had the rank in case I needed it.

14 January — Quite an uneventful day. Have been reading an Ellery Queen mystery, attended a show at the airdrome theater and got soaking wet. Some of the boys went out this morning.

17 January — Same as yesterday [*nothing, just waiting*]. We're teasing the Bell [*P-39*] man [*the factory representative, to put in a*] "forgettor switch," [*something to remind us of the procedures*] . . . . The latest rumor — Bury the tale [*tail*] of the P-39 in a block of cement & use it for an antiaircraft gun! [*The P-39 nose had a big .37mm cannon in it, and with the tail buried, the boys thought the aircraft would make a great antiaircraft gun!*] Bought a new pen today & sold my old one. The weather isn't bad here. This is a very nice island and after the war it will be something that can be developed to great advantage . . . former fellow cadet is flying B-24s. Wishes he could fly pursuit. I don't blame him! . . .

18 January — Today completes my first month overseas! Time isn't going too slow. Awakened at 03:30 to board "Scat" [*C-47 transport*] flights, called off. . . . Wind and rain grew terrifically. I was in the sack when the roof blew off. Moved to the next one and it went too. Finally went to the latrine. That was the safest place. The mess hall also had been damaged. It died down as suddenly as it came — and everyone was wet!

20 January — Has been a nice hot day. We leave for the Russells [*in the*

Solomons] tomorrow. . . . Drew parachute etc. Got unpacked in time to get packed again!

23 January — Flew 3 hrs today. . . . No Restrictions — Hooray. . . .

24 January — Flew with Capt Street this morning. Was to go up with him again but ear trouble prevented it. He seemed well enough pleased with my flying. Poor Bruce got it again — but thank goodness he wasn't hurt. He has the worst luck of anyone I know. Brakes this time!

27 January — Raining pretty hard — it rains here all of the time. Live in a cocoanut grove. I would surely hate to stay here — Mud is about as hard on morale as a good old New Mexico dust storm! . . .

28 January — Friday — Arrived on Ondonga [*island in the northern Solomon Islands*] — this is the best place I have seen since I have been overseas. Especially good after being in the Russells. Coral runways — roadways & paths. Live in swell Quonset huts with sheets, mattress & bed-spreads!! Have a book shelf on which I put Elvena's picture — all the comforts of home! Hot & cold showers & even a good latrine! Combat missions start here!

30 January — Got up at 04:30 this morning, took off on dawn patrol to Torokina [*airstrip on Bougainville*]. Flew 7:55 min. Not tired though [*I do not show how many missions this involved.*] Scramble alert [*called an "S.A"; we sit near our planes until the siren goes off, then take off in a hurry to check it out*] & patrol. Ran into tropical storm on the way "home." Took a chance & came thru it anyway. [*The day before I had flown six hours. Usually we flew several short missions in a day and then skipped a day or two.*]

31 January — Today off — slept & ate all day. . . . Beautiful morning but rained all afternoon. It rains here everyday.

The crew here are very good — a far cry to some that I had met in the Russells — they were strictly off the ball. The planes here are in excellent shape, however one of the crew chiefs told me today that he didn't know what they would do for spare parts if we didn't crack one up now and then. I told him that I wouldn't like to accommodate them!

IN FEBRUARY 1944 we were in the Solomon Islands. The way it was then our flight (four of us) lived in one tent together and stayed together about all the time. This presumably helped scheduling. It was well organized and I liked my flight very much — Captain Worley, Lieutenant Mills, Lieutenant Harvey L. Harvey, and myself.

One of my first combat missions was to bomb and strafe a spot in the jungle, but with my untrained eye I could see nothing down there. But by watching Captain Worley, I did almost everything exactly as he did by dropping my bomb and strafing, etc. The Coast Watchers said there were 100 dead Japanese scattered all over the place.

Our Coast Watchers were Australians and some natives. They performed outstanding feats of bravery, reporting by radio or messenger the troops, ships, planes, and movements of the enemy, which would give us warnings of attacks or places to attack.

5 February 1944 — Everything OK. Strafed Shortland [*Island*] and patrolled at Torokina [*on Bougainville*]. Nothing very exciting. Asked for an exchange in ships as "The Mrs" and I just didn't get along too well. A good ship, but landed differently than I had been used to.

7 February — Took off at dawn & stood S.A. at Treasury [*Island*]. We were scrambled but no luck. Received about 20 letters today and it really helped out a lot. There were several accidents today, but all OK.

9 February — Stood scramble alert today & flew only dawn & dusk patrol. I am crazy about my ship & the crew chief seems quite eager. I think I should have Elvena's name put on it because it is so sweet.

13 February — Last night I experienced my first real air raid. Bombs hit in Ondonga and Munda [*on New Georgia in the Solomons*]. Could hear the bombs fall with a "swoosh." Every one sounded like it was coming in the foxhole & the next one sounded a little bit closer! Destroyed 14 trucks —

no casualties. [*"Shod" Eugene*] Pischke was still in the sack when the first one hit. He and [*Ben*] Jones almost made another opening to the foxhole. Arrived at Torokina today & went almost to front lines with Capt Worley to visit his friend in the Americal Division.

14 February — Flew over six hours today but nothing happened. Tomorrow is the big day! . . .

15 February — Today took off at dark this morning. Patrolled landing of Task Force on Green Island. [*These missions required us to circle over a task force of ships in case the enemy sent in bombers.*] No sooner than we got on station when Jap dive bombers attacked. The task force really put up the flak. It looked so pretty coming up all around — until it got too close for comfort. . . . Fred [*Belue*] came in for belly landing; we were scrambled late this evening. Negative.

OUR NAVY WAS FIRING ON US, so we changed locations in a hurry. The whole landing went off really well, but it was a Marine and Navy show, and our group was more or less to stand by in case they needed us. There weren't many Japanese planes,and I think they were all shot down. I was disappointed that we couldn't get in on the action. We were assigned a certain area to orbit, and that is what we did — they really hadn't needed us at all. Later we made a lot of ground support missions over Green Island, bombing and strafing.

17 February — I flew well over seven hours today [*My log does not say how many missions; later I kept better track.*] — Dumbo Escort [a PBY *rescue plane*] and we went well up in the St. George[*'s*] Channel [*north of New Britain near Rabaul*]. . . . Dumbo really should get an awful lot of credit and praise, because they are at the mercy of the Japs [*pilots and gun-*

ners] in the event they are discovered. [*The Rescue Squadron picked up many downed pilots throughout the war.*]

19 February — We covered a task force to G. [*Green*] Island today. Negative. Got along fine. After we came down Capt Worley and Harvey, Mills and myself went to the beach. . . . sandy only the sand is blackish. At first sight it looks dirty, but it is very clean. . . . Some new P-40 pilot landed along the runway last night until he came to the end of it. He went right on off into the "drink." He wasn't hurt but of course the plane was demolished. . . . I had a silly dream last night — I became the papa of a baby born with his oxygen mask on and wearing a silly looking dress or something. I sure haven't been sleeping well lately. The night before I dreamed about a rattlesnake. (That should make me more homesick than scared!!). . . .

20 February — Sunday: Today was another day off for me. . . . Jones went in the drink this morning, but he is OK I think — a destroyer picked him up. . . . Later: Jones had a fractured back or something. Had to be sent home — grounded for 8 months.

21 February — . . . went on a mission with Col. Wilmot. Just the two of us went. We were to dive bomb and strafe a Jap bivouac area. . . . I made a direct hit on the 2nd hut — pulled up and went around. My bomb did not explode immediately but when the Col. came around the bomb went off. There was a big fire. . . . The engine was terribly rough after the last pass and I "sweated out" getting home. I came in "low and slow" — the Col hovered about and saw that I landed OK. . . .

22 February — Ferry and patrol and tracking today. . . . Capt. Smith — a fellow I knew who had flown in the AVG's went down today — crash landed at Torokina. Also Lt. [*Dick*] Brown of our Sqdn disappeared — I am waiting to hear the latest about him — he was the hottest pilot I believe in our outfit and a swell fellow too. Eight more days and he would get to go home. That really seems bad. [*I saw this happen all too often that a pilot would go down just before his time to go home.*] . . . The artillery is pounding away tonight. We expect an invasion attempt or something — that came from a prisoner up in the Americal division.

23 February — Patrolled over Green Isle. Then we dive bombed and strafed a couple of barges. Both barges were sunk. Then we strafed some areas where the Japs were bivouaced. They still haven't located Captain Brown. . .

26 February — . . . took a ship up [*during*] Slow-time. This was a lot of fun as it was the first time since I have been overseas that I have been up by myself. . . .

27 February — Flew this morning on an interesting mission. One of the flight leaders didn't want to go so I took his place. I was standing S.A. at the time. We took 500# bombs up and went on a "search." Shoot up & bomb anything we could find. Lt. Workman spotted a pillbox . . . I released my bomb right where I had intended to and it hit exactly where I had intended. I was pleased. . . as it means that at least I have gotten back in the groove in dive bombing. (Skip bombing is my dish though) . . . [*Skip bombing is when you come in with a shallow dive with a delayed-action fuse bomb. You get very low and make like you are going to fly through the door of the building, release the bomb and peel up; the bomb hits the ground, skips slightly, ends up in the building, and goes off.*]

28 February — . . . I spent most of the day trying to make some kind of trinket and finally bungled it all up as usual so gave up. . . . Lt. Artwhol went in the drink — prop went out I guess. He was picked up immediately by a crash boat. Heard Ben [*Jones*] is in Guadalcanal in the hospital (back injury).

29 February — I was quite eager today and did quite a bit of test hopping — boy was that fun! . . . attended a lecture tonight. . . . Won't be here much longer. . . .

1 March 1944 — Had a couple of missions today — bombed & strafed [*M*]anitou [*M*]ission [*a Japanese installation*] — I flew a Q-15 [*P-39Q-15*] again today . . . but it takes a bit of time to get back to using the synchronized prop & throttle control. . . . On last mission I came in in the Q15 & just couldn't get it down. I ballooned 5 or 6 feet so I just decided to go around. . . . That is about the third time I have done this. . . . Sgt French is visiting us tonight — he is Major Worley's friend from the Americal div.

We had a big egg fry tonight. Boy were they good. . . . I ate four eggs and drank a lot of coffee. I think our new C.O. has come in. Major [*Leonard*] Shapiro replacing Col. Wilmot. . . .

2 March — . . . We have just been relieved & will move out immediately.
Later: We did move out in an awful hurry. Arrived here in Guadalcanal this evening. It is very hot tonight. . . .

3 March — . . . I went to see Ben, a swell fellow and a good pilot. Tears rolled down his face when told that he could no longer be with us. Since he can't be able to fly for the next 6 or eight months he will be sent back to the States. I am glad that he can go back now that this has happened. . . .

4 March — Still waiting. . . . I hate to move around so much. I would much sooner be in Torokina than here. Of course I guess I will enjoy Auckland if we get there. . . . I tried to check out in a P-38 this morning, but there was a shortage of them here.

8 March — Left today by PBM — 9 hrs to Auckland. . . . What a beautiful place.

10 March — Left for the Coates farm in Matakohe [*Matakohe, North Island, New Zealand*] some hundred miles away. I enjoyed the train ride very much & it was thru beautiful mountain country covered with clean little farms. . . . We arrived at the home where I was to stay. What a beautiful home. . . I later met the rest of the family. . . . They were all swell to me.

WE WERE SENT ON A rest leave (R&R) to Auckland, New Zealand, where the squadron had rented a house. Some played poker and partied, but this did not suit my style, especially after having been recently married. The Red Cross said they had a place for me, and shipped me to Metakohe, to the Coates Station (Ranch).

The Coates family was so nice to me; they wouldn't let me spend a cent.

I guess they treated other soldiers the same way. I tried to help out as much as possible. The family would stop and have tea at 10:00 a.m. and 3:00 p.m., as well as with any company stopping by in between. Mr. Coates said that I looked puny, and he had me drink a shot of whiskey with milk each night at 10 o'clock. I learned later that he was a member of parliament and his brother was the Prime Minister of New Zealand.

The Coates family wrote letters to my wife and my folks throughout the war. They really appreciated the Yanks because we turned back the Japanese navy, which was coming down to land on New Guinea, Australia, and New Zealand, at the Battle of the Coral Sea. Mr. Coates very kindly told me to bring my wife back to New Zealand and they would set us up. But we never did get there.

It was interesting to watch the New Zealanders work cattle and sheep with their very intelligent and efficient dogs. An animal could be selected for removal from the herd, and the dogs would isolate it, take it over to another corner. There was no shouting; it was all very quietly done.

I will always remember the kindness and hospitality of the Coates family to a lonely serviceman away from home.

There was some sort of statistic put out by the Red Cross that an average flying officer on rest leave was 24 years old, unmarried, and a high school graduate with probably a year of two of college. He was weary, but had a very good attitude about wanting to finish the war. He had flown about 600 hours in military aircraft, had been on 21 missions, and was in good physical condition.

I was then 23 years old and just married, but fit most of the other statistics.

21 March — Arrived in Guadalcanal today. Nothing eventful has happened. I was ready to come back but dread going to the Russells.

22 March — Were to leave today, went down to the most inefficient Scat office and they had called the flight off. . . . It is now 1st Lt. A.C. . . . I just learned some news from the old 85th. Rodriquez was killed in a P-48. I surely hated to hear that. I liked him very much. . . .

23 March — Heard that Major Collins went in (Rabaul) — Tail came off. A fine fellow & pilot.

25 March — Arrived in Russells. . . . Easy Knight [*from our squadron*] went in yesterday. . . . Letter from Red [*Garrison, who had been best man at my wedding*] today said that F/O Collins was killed in his first overseas flight. There were several others missing but in other sqdns. . . . Have 14 new fellows in Sqdn.

26 March — Stood scramble alert today. Flew one mission with one of the new fellows. He seems OK.

27 March — Flew tracking mission today then flew to Guadalcanal. . . . They have been contemplating sending home some of our squadron. Gee I'll be glad for them. . . . I really feel good now that I am back flying. . . . Pilot's meeting tonight — big "chewing." I guess some hot rock bomber pilot came over to check out in our P-39's — result, one less P-39 & a messed up runway. Hard luck. [*Lieutenant Wilfred*] Henkey bellied in while taxiing — sat right down on a depth charge — a nice way to keep from growing old!!

29 March — Spent the morning making out accident reports — rather, I was just learning. . . . (accident investigation committee). Played volleyball again — and of course the usual rain. . . . 10 pilots & navigators still missing from the 75th Bomb [*Squadron*]. . . .

30 March — Dive bombed today — rat race afterward. I led the second element. I am now official Sqdn Test Pilot. That makes two jobs I have. . . . I shall be busy enough. . . . Freddie landed over at the other strip by mistake.

1 April 1944 — Took dawn patrol this morning on search for that sub. Still haven't made contact with it. Pischke and I are out to get that thing if we can. I have been begging for an airplane for tonight: don't know whether we will get it or not. The sub should surface somewhere around. I surely would like to catch him surfaced.

2 April — Today is Sunday — had a tooth ground down & an Xray of the piece of iron or steel in my finger. . . . This afternoon I went over to the other strip & ferried a plane back over here. There had been water in the distributor & the battery had run down. . . .

3 April — Went to another intelligence meeting — then flew as element leader in Harvey's flight on a dive bombing mission. He really gave us a workout. We had our pictures taken this afternoon. . . . I went on a test hop for carburation [*sic*] — the left brake gave completely out when I took off. Had to cut mixture and switches when landing — and managed to come out OK on a taxi strip. This morning Cunningham's brake gave out and he went into the ditch . . . the Major was hot on the case of taxi accidents [*moving planes on the ground*]. . . . Schaffer bailed out. He is O.K. Plane was on fire. . . .

4 April — . . . Later today I had a couple of test hops. Did some acrobatics [*sic*] — fell out of my slow rolls terribly bad. Will have to practice for awhile. . . . This morning I landed with no flaps. . . awfully "hot." . . . I managed to sneak off with a bomb on one test flight. — I dive bombed a tiny island & hit it squarely in the center! . . . I am now Element Leader in the Major's flight.

5 April — Here in Ondonga now. Gee it was surely good to get back here where the chow is better, hot showers, barber shops, tailor shops, shoe shops, sheets & bedspreads & mattresses. Room orderlies who clean the room up every day. The Quonset huts are very nice inside — What more could we want! There are only about five flights here — not many planes — but good ones, what there are. Q-6s here.

9 April — . . . After dinner I flew (co-pilot) a U.C. [*Utility Cargo*] 78 (Cessna [*Bobcat, light transport trainer*]) for 40 minutes. It is the first twin engine ship I have flown.

11 April — Flew to the Russells this morning and attended to some things in the way of accident reports etc.

14 April — . . . Twelve fellows out of the squadron are going home. . . Oh lucky boys, and I am glad for them. . . . They called me & told me that I had a bad tire and to use caution.

Edwin R. ("Junior") Cunningham, the youngest pilot in the 68th Fighter Squadron. He survived combat, but was killed in a plane crash in the States.

15 April — Had a lot of fun when I went up with the C.O. Major Shapiro in a dive bomb mission. He flew my wing. . . . He is a good guy.

ON 15 APRIL 1944, our new Commanding Officer, Major Leonard Shapiro, joined us on his first dive bomb mission with our 68th Squadron. Instead of leading, he chose to fly as my wing man — now that is something for a commanding officer to do. When we landed he said he made a sorry wing man but he did his best. We sure laughed. He was something else; I liked him from the start.

We flew many dive bombing and strafing missions. Once on a test hop, the nose gearbox sprayed oil all over my windshield, and I could hardly see to land in the rain.

Bill Gaskill in front of a P-39. The bandage on the neck is a throat-mike burn.

17 April — Dive bomb & strafe. Worley & [*Lieutenant Bob*] Morriss both in the hospital. That really knocks a hole in our flight.

20 April — Last night a searchlight tracking mission came up and it was given to me. Well, this is no field for night landings. It was a very interesting mission. The searchlights, when shined upon me, would give me the awfullest [*sic*] feeling of vertigo, I was on instruments most all the time anyway as I couldn't see the horizon all of the time. I came in to land. I said I would make several passes at the field and if I couldn't make it, I would go to Munda. Instead, though, I flew it right into the ground and held it there. The only time I was lost was when I was turning off the runway; then I couldn't find the taxi strip! The "Blue Ops" were well pleased and certainly did appreciate it. The pleasure was theirs!!!

23 April — . . . New boys arrived in Sqdn. Received. . . a letter from Red. . . . Red is in Oahu.

27 April — Flew L-1-C [*Stinson Vigilant, ambulance/liaison plane*] today and took up crew chiefs & went after mail to Munda. Had more fun with it! Stalls below 18 mph, cruises about 90 or less (80) and can dive it to 150, I guess. Had rather fly it than C-78 or L4A [*Piper Cub Grasshopper, trainer and light liaison plane*]. No flying otherwise. . . . Ran into Copeland — good old "Copey" from primary. He is now navigator in SCAT. Surely glad to see him. . . . Was given a "talking to" this morning from Major Worley. He gave me some very good advice and I surely appreciated it — it was about something an officer should know and do and some things I could do to improve myself as an officer . . . that I should show more authority. . . .

29 April — . . . have a bad mike burn, also some heat rash. [*I suffered a mike burn on my neck which became badly infected; then the jungle rot spread down my front before we could stop it.*]

1 May 1944 — Strafed today — got mail in Munda. Then this afternoon I checked out in the plane that I always wanted to fly — P-38H. It really was the most exciting, thrilling thing that has happened to me — lately. Twenty minutes after I took off I felt at home in it and did 6 rolls to the left and one to the right — then buzzed the runway and went buzzing all around. These planes are coming to the 70th [*Squadron*]. Flying that ship is a thrill — more power, more speed — but a wee bit too much like a bomber. Came in [*to land*] at about 110 mph — leveled off over runway at 100 and was too hot [*fast*], but set down okay. It was too short a field to be checking out on — but I got along fine. The landing wasn't bad, leveled off a bit too high. The thing stalls beautifully with none of this unstable feeling that one gets in the P-39. There are surely a lot more things to do in this ship [*since it had twice the instruments and twice the procedures, etc. The P-38 was our first fighter that could fly over 400 mph.*].

3 May — Still waiting — impatiently. Left Ondonga in P-39s and arrived in Torokina. Flew a combat mission after arriving here, a test hop. . . .

6 May — Most interesting day. We took off to bomb New Britain (Talili). My wheels would not come up; the toggle switch broke. I decided to crank them up and that was the awfullest job. I cranked and cranked trying to stay in formation at the same time. The darn manual control would bind. . . . Worley motioned for me to go. I shook my head. He said well crank them up then. . . . Perspiration pouring down my face getting in my eyes. And Major Worley laughing at me! I was determined to go through. . . . [*I had to crank them down again at Green Island where we landed and refueled. They fixed the switches and loaded incendiary bombs.*] I think I made a good hit. . . . Half a dozen or more ships have been hit by ack ack [*anti-aircraft fire — AA*].

7 May — Cunningham in our flight hit a tree. Owens also hit a tree. A P-40 pilot hit a tree today and was killed. Shaeffer's plane was badly shot up today. I have been kept busy with the test hops in addition to my regular flying. Today we had two dive bomb missions. Have been hitting pretty well lately. Early our flight hit a village and just blew the place all up. Cunningham's bomb blew bits of roof and debris high into the air. We all made direct hits in the area. He said mine (bomb) almost shook his teeth out. . . . Morriss and Cunningham are both new boys . . . they are turning out quite well. . . . [*We*] have been dropping the bombs at too low an altitude resulting in being hit by shrapnel from our own bombs . . . the other day I was testing one for a new wing installed so I took it up to 15,000 and started into a dive. At about 300 mph cowling underneath ripped off. I thought sure the tail had come off and was surely ready to jump. [*Any time we had a structural replacement I had to really wring the plane out. Sometimes it left me tired all over.*]

10 May — . . . We are flying Q-6's, Q-15's, Q-20's & Q-5's, about 39 planes with at least 30 in commission all the time. Excellent maintenance here and I am glad.

12 May — Best mission yet! Strafed right in Simpson Harbor [*Rabaul*]. We followed some (88) bombers. (Strafed many boats & barges) The sky was full of stuff. They threw up everything but the kitchen sink!! & then we came in right behind the bombers at tree top level & dropped down right on the shore. We had terrific speed & had throttle in. . . . We must have come in at nearly 380 and I throttled back and fired at about 300 mph, then full throttle & evasive action . . . we got safely out of there and no one was hit. . . . First P-39's to strafe Rabaul!! It was announced over the radio that we had sunk or damaged 30-40 Jap barges & vessels. Divide that by 12 & I got my share of them!! . . . But: ComAirSols counted on losing at least 3 P-39s. . . . [*We lost none. I was told that Major Shapiro had tears in his eyes when he scheduled that mission. He thought he would lose most of us. There was certainly a lot of ack-ack and guns and cannons fired at us. I don't know how the enemy could have missed us.*]

Friday the 13th! . . . Had dawn patrol — the sunrise was beautiful this morning. It was cold up at angels 10 [*code name for 10,000 feet*]. But we turned on the heaters and were so comfortable. That is about the best mission (patrol) of the day as the weather is perfect — the air smooth and stable. . .

14 May — Went to Vunakanau [*Japanese airfield in the Solomon Islands*] — twenty-four of us. . . . AA was heavy and intense, but inaccurate. . . . Started our dives at about 14,000 and pulled out at about 7,000. . . . No one was hit — but one — Brannon's door was warped and opened by AA concussion.

15 May — Took a Q-1 [*P-39Q-10*] up to 29,000' this morning on a test hop. [*The P-39 was really sick — sloppy on the controls — at that altitude.*] . . .

16 May — Another beautiful direct hit on the Japs! . . . While on the first mission, for some reason or another, our Coastal Artillery threw a bit of ack ack right at us and it was accurate too. . . . We have been told — and I really and truly believe, that we have the best — at least one of the best

— flights in the Sqdn. [*That made me very happy.*] . . . it was Major Worley's constant diligence while in training. . . . Cunningham is one of the best flyers that I have seen . . . and Morriss is just plenty all right too. . . . Worley shot up his prop strafing [*Two of his machine guns got out of time with his propeller.*] and is really lucky to get home. . . . Cox blew tire on T.O [*takeoff*]. . . . I should like to fly the rest of my combat time out here just like I am now! And so ends the day with a few less Japs on Bougainville — I hope!

17 May — To Vunakanau again this morning. When we left Green I[*sland*] Major Worley noticed that his gas tanks had not been filled. He and Cunningham returned, also Lt. Cox. My airspeed [*indicator*] was out all the way but I went anyway. [*That is not usually done!*] Morriss's door sprung open. All in all that was the most screwed up flight I had been on in a long time. . . . Lt. Love took off too close and too low airspeed this morning — he sucked up his wheels and he just settled right back on the runway — dropped a wing and crash landed on his incendiary bomb. Boy, of all the fire works! It looked like the fourth of July!! He wasn't injured — miraculously — the plane was a total wreck. Better days ahead — I hope!! [*We had to wait on the taxi strips until they could bulldoze the mess out of the way. He went over, crawled in another plane that was ready, and rejoined the mission. He was one lucky boy.*] . . . This evening I tangled with a P-38 while I was on a test hop. It was quite a battle. I outmaneuvered, out climbed, out accelerated and out dived him [*practicing*]. . . .

18 May — Had two test flights. The first was another acceptance check. I really did wring it out, diving at a little over 500 mph. [*Strangely, a P-39 was safer than a P-38 after you exceeded 500 mph.*] . . . This evening Morriss and I took off on a very important mission. Three hidden camouflaged barges in Chabai. The weather was poor so we were handicapped and dropped our bombs at a dangerously low altitude. Then we strafed . . . I dropped on the target — a direct hit and Morriss and I got two barges and one damaged. . . . There was a big oil slick on the water when we left!! . . . I will leave for Auckland in about three weeks. Sam Wallis and McBride had a midair collision, but neither of them were hurt. [*Miracles happen.*] . . . Tonight while sitting here, there was a slight tremor. We are sitting off to one side of two volcanoes. . . They are active and dense white smoke pours out all day long. One night after we went to bed there was quite a little earthquake.

19 May — Dive bombed the Duke of York island. . . . Two planes were badly shot up today. Good mission [*scheduled*] tomorrow.

20 May — Went to Kahili on a coordinated strike. We (our flight) was the first one over and did we get the A.A. — really did use evasive action and I flew out of there at tree top level. . . . Tomorrow morning I go to Green to pick up and test a ship, then go on the strike to Vunakanau — maybe!

21 May — Went via that darn "Scat" to Green Island and picked up No. 106 [*P-39*]. I had to test hop it first as the gear box should have been changed. Had to test it again this evening and tangled with a P-38 again [*in a mock dogfight*]. . . .

22 May — Was supposed to go to Rabaul — just before we got there Jr.'s [*Cunningham's*] ship began giving much trouble so he and I returned to Green. I stayed there and Rowe and I flew two crippled ships home this afternoon. I really sweated Jr. out this morning as I felt quite responsible for his safety — I shouldn't have let him take off from Green with the plane in the shape it was. Rowe and I ran into weather on the way back and darned if I didn't nearly spin in on the approach — it was raining and I really did slip-skid and what have you to get in. I didn't want to go around as I probably couldn't anyway. The motor could cut out at 30 HG [*inches of mercury, or "boost"*]. Had a test hop later this afternoon and everything was wrong with the plane so it seemed. Gyro out, relay [*electrical*], l.g.[*landing gear*] out, alti [*altimeter*] out, radio out. Golly, what a day. Was informed tonight that I would be grounded as I had too much time (highest in the Sqdn.). That would be hard to take. Of course I could have regular test hops etc. — but won't get any good missions. Sun & Sever's flights returned tonight — they got as far as G.canal [*Guadalcanal*] and all leaves to Auckland were canceled — something is up!!! I guess there won't be any more trips to Auckland — but to Australia instead!!

23 May — We went in to dive bomb positions in Rabaul. . . . We dived from 13,000 to 1,000 . . . the cockpit fogged up. . . . As I pulled off the target they had me boresighted — I turned to join with Major Worley and a stream of bullets whizzed past and dropped in front and to the left of me. I whipped over to the right and there was another long burst. Boy I really was sweating that out. . . . Then I had some test hops. Five hours today.

24 May — Today I am 23 years of age. . . . Cunningham had trouble with his engine again. . . . I have test hopped it several times. . . . Last night Lt. Love D[*ive*]. B[*ombed*]. a float plane in Buka and they got him too.

25 May — Received many letters from home . . . my name has been plastered all over the local weekly papers just because of the air medal and clusters. . . . Lt's. Hackbarth, Swanson, and Comstock have all met tragic endings. They were such swell fellows. . . . we had a mission which was a show [*formation*] for Admiral Halsey: I hope he enjoyed it because we surely didn't. The Navy was late [*we nearly ran out of gas*]. . . .

26 May — . . . we bombed Chabai in close formation at 1100 ft. and we really felt the bombs go off too! [*We were coming in too low for that kind of instantaneous fused bomb.*]. . . .

27 May — . . . Major Worley and several others [*and I*] went out and located [*Lieutenant*] McBee's grave and reburied the boy with a formal but simple funeral service. The major blew taps. There was a guard of honor and everything. . . came pretty close to spinning in out of a loop. Had me quite worried for awhile, but finally fell out of it after losing a lot of altitude! <u>Resolved</u>: I am going to stop flyin' around in a "fog" [*making so many mistakes*]. [*Claud V.*] McLemore was hit by flack — only a slight injury. [*Lieutenant John*] Skinner's plane was also shot up.

28 May — Today was a royally screwed up deal. As we left the target, Tobera airfield, Cunningham lost Worley. From there on everyone was lost. We finally formed again — some never did get back with their own flights. None of us was hit — but an S.B.D. [*Douglas Dauntless Navy dive bomber*] was shot down (not an uncommon occurrence). Worley was so chipped off that we did acrobatics half the way home. He always does do acrobatics after we have goofed off; by that way we can always tell when he is disgruntled. . . .

29 May — . . . This rather unlucky day for the 68th. Lt. Olson went in the drink northeast of the island — but was picked up — he is okay. Lt. Goggins — at approximately the same time disappeared suddenly while on a strafing mission. That is very mysterious — it is possible that he hit a tree because he disappeared so suddenly. A wing bomb fell off on the runway tearing up a wing. (Two planes and pilots missing with one also damaged.) Lt. Pritchard is going to be sent home. He had a pretty close "call" I guess. He has been in the hospital over a month. . . .

31 May — Today I tested two ships. . . . Had a bit of trouble with [*one*]. The [*cockpit*] door sprung open in a dive. What a racket!!. . . Late this evening Morriss and I took the dusk sweep. . . . We both got good hits — mine in a supply area . . . and his on some barges in Buka Passage [*north of Bougainville*]. . . . It was getting dark and the tracers looked beautiful. We had our navigation lights on so we could see each other. Being so low to the ground it is quite easy to get separated. . . . We saw and inspected some natives and huts . . . but they appeared to be friendly so we left them alone. . . . Have a bad cold. . . . Ear was quite painful when I made my run on the target. . . .

1 June 1944 — . . . Tonight Morriss, Cunningham, and myself . . . spotted . . . a gun position . . . which was really firing at us and came very close to each of us in our bombing dive. I . . . climbed up to 5,000' and waited for them. Then I started to make another run on the target. When I started my dive and then spotted this gunboat, I changed course and released [*my bomb*] at 1,200 — a direct hit!! It blew up and burned with a very large orange flame with black smoke. . . . M & C said the tracers were peppering away at me. . . . Later today a mechanic came up to me and said "did you see 125 — the pilot that flew that last night nearly didn't get back." I nearly fell over. I ran over and there they were changing the engine on it. A fifty caliber or something had torn out one spark plug & blast tube and splattered around here and there. There were two more holes in the empennage [*tail*]. Now they tell me!!

Had a four hour lecture on operation of P-38's. Then I had a short test hop.

4 June — Major Worley checked out in one of our new 38's — he crash landed on the Piva strip. . . . Hydraulics system went out. . . .

5 June — . . . we were landing after the strike to Rabaul when some Corsairs [*F4U, Navy*] broke or tried to break in between our and [*Lieutenant Stephen J.*] Sun's flights. . . . I was crowded out and had to break sharply away to the right to avoid a collision. . . . I had to go around, Cunningham also. . . . Worley emergency landed at ocean tower [*another parallel airstrip*] because of being low on gas. . . . We . . . wrote up the thing in a formal statement. Major Worley advised disciplinary action. [*I don't know what ever came of it. Nobody was hurt in the episode.*]

6 June — **<u>Invasion of France</u>** — [*But meanwhile in the Pacific*] we dive bombed and strafed trucks and guns on a road. They were shooting at us. We — or rather the New Zealanders and we destroyed many guns and vehicles. . . .

7 June — . . . The whole day has been rather bad, but the news from the European theater is swell. Six more P-38's. Hooray, or is it!! Also [*it's now*] <u>1st Lt</u> Morriss, I am glad for him too. He deserved it!!

8 June — Checked out again in a P-38: guess we will begin to get a little time in them every day now. . . . About the P-38 — it is a man-sized job to handle it, but you are safe in it — no whip stalls, high speed stalls, spins, . . . but it is like trying to drive a big truck after having driven a Ford! In a dive it really picks up speed. . . . It will cruise at 250 [*mph*] at 30" to 35" [*of boost*]. It is strictly a rudder ship — but it really takes the strength to coordinate it properly. There is four times as much to check in it as there was in our 39. Consequently it takes alot longer to get started and get off the ground. [*The heavy handling of the P-38 was corrected when hydraulic boosters were installed on the controls — that really changed things.*] . . . Oh well, I guess it will be okay after we get use to it. That is the way it is with any ship — we don't like it until we get use to the new thing. . . .

9 June — Flew 5 hrs 15 min today, but am not tired tonight . . . had to test 106 again for the third time in two days. . . . First detonation — now overheating. Took off and couldn't get my wheels up. . . . Our foot lockers came today. It's only been on the way seven months too! I opened my Christmas presents which Elvena had given me before I left the states. [*My foot locker also contained winter underwear and a heavy overcoat! I got* *them out and paraded up and down the company street in the tropical heat. I believe they were about ready to give me a "Section 8," for guys who go berserk.*] . . .

10 June — Went to Rabaul, but . . . Morriss's engine began giving trouble and so he and I returned to Green. His cockpit was splattered and the floor covered with black oil. I surely thought he was going to have to get out and swim. Coming back from Green . . . Worley motioned for me to get rid of my bomb. I knew I had dropped it on the target but he kept motioning for me so I thought I had a hung bomb [*one that wouldn't release*]. I pulled back on the bomb release and yanked back on the stick. I really racked it around [*trying all the while to pull my manual release*]. In the meantime Cunningham ran off and left me. . . . When I caught up with them they cut their throttles. I went into the awfullest skids & slips and everything trying to get into formation. . . . What a joke to play when coming back from a combat mission. . . . They all got a kick out of it though. [*I didn't have a bomb on, but you can't tell from inside the cockpit.*]

11 June — Went direct to Rabaul — the most AA I believe I have encountered. Later on afternoon sweep one of our P-38s crashed & burned on Piva [*on Bougainville*], pilot O.K.

12 June — Spent the whole day at SCAT waiting to go to Green Isle for No. 106 — negative. . . . Ran into Col. Milton and I was very glad to see him and he seemed surprised and rather glad to see me. [*He had been president of the New Mexico A & M College when I last saw him. He wrote my mother that we knelt and prayed for a good old New Mexico sand storm. He was quite a guy.*] Pretty blue tonight as things have not turned out as they should. I am disappointed and discouraged. Cox returned from his honeymoon! [*George L.*] Mayberry was shot down but he was picked up okay. Has ten stitches in his face and head: from the gun sight. He water landed. Note: always keep Sutton [*safety*] Harness on in a plane.

13 June — Went to Rabaul today. . . . [*I made a bad approach.*] Went around at Green . . . . I was making what I thought was a good approach & landing when all of a sudden I hit the road, along the beach, just before you strike the mat. I hit that road and bounced back up about 15 feet. That was the hardest landing I ever made. I hit my head against the canopy and raised a knot — I still have a headache. . . . My flying hasn't been improving any lately. Got another '38 today — a J-5. Major Shapiro was standing in front of operations and saw what I did. He patted me on the back and said "we all make a bad landing now and then." He said that he was glad that I went around as it showed I saw and admitted my mistake so went around and corrected it. . . .

14 June — Went to Rabaul today. . . . Morriss and 18 others ferried planes [*P-39s*] to G.canal and will bring back P-38s (J-15s, I hope!). . . Oh yes. Strafed a Jap "Johnny house" [*latrine*] and filled it full (of lead). . . . That was "dirty" but fun.

15 June — Checked out again in P-38. . . . Generator and amp meter went out. . . . Tonight they are celebrating Worley's 28th birthday. . . .

16 June — Went to Rabaul for the last time in P-39s, I hope. When we came back we flew (Junior and I) the P-38 for about hour and a half. . . . There was an assignment of flights tonight. I believe our flight has been changed to Capt [*John*] Stege [*our new Commanding Officer*] — new fellow, but an experienced combat pilot [*in the North African Theater*]. He is a swell fellow and everyone seems to like him very much. Still and all Major Worley is hard to beat and we hate to lose him as a flight leader. . . . His [*new*] duties require all of his time. Capt Stege is also the assistant operations officer. On the strike to Rabaul I led Lt. Sun's element and we got along fine. I like to fly with him very much, but after Jr. and I have been flying with other flights — it really made us appreciate our own. One of the fellows really lagged behind and just wouldn't close up. It not only looked slouchy, but had we been jumped he would have been a dead "duck" as naturally stragglers are always picked off first and we could never have gotten to him in time. . . .

17 June — Flew formation with Major Worley today. It then broke up and we had a swell rat race only I wasn't enough on the ball to do much good. Did a formation loop but I fell out of it — what a dope!

18 June — Flew one P-38 test hop. I am the assistant test pilot with or to Lt. Hernden. He is an "old" P-38 pilot and has a lot of knowledge on engines etc. I will probably learn a lot about a P-38 from him. [*The assis-*

124 PASSENGERS | REMARKS

17 June Flew formation with
Major Worley today. It then
broke up and we had a swell
rat race only I wasn't
enough on the ball to
do much good. Did a
formation loop but I fell
out of it - what a dope!
18 June Flew one P-38 test
hop - I am the assistant test
pilot with or to Lt. Hernden. He
is an 'old' P38 pilot and has a
lot of knowledge on engines etc.
I will probably learn a lot about
a P-38 from him. McLean -
Sever - Mathews - Rupp → USA
19 June We flew two hours
formation with our new
flight leader and really enjoyed
it. Shimmer took my
place Bryant's landing gear

16—18016 GPO

The Aviators Flight Log Book entry for 18 June 1944.

tant does most all the work anyway. The main reason I was test pilot was because I don't play poker and being around the flight line a lot I just naturally fell into that job.] McLemore, Sever, Mathews, Rupp to USA.

19 June — . . . Bryant's landing gear folded up on landing — he did not lock it before he landed. The plane swerved off the runway and hit a truck — the truck was completely demolished and the plane was pretty well torn up. Bryant was not injured — lucky! Went over to visit the native village taken over by our gov't. The population is about 1,200. . . . They come from all over the island and are half starved. They get food and shelter within our perimeter. . . . They tend a large garden. . . . They build their own huts with the aid of, I suppose, the Engineers. The huts look quite nice too. They are of assorted shapes and colors — saw some of them smoking who don't appear to be over three or four years of age. [*The children and women carried heavy loads of supplies and the old men followed behind carrying a walking stick!*]

20 June — . . . Pischke had a close one today when he forgot to put his wheels down on a single engine landing — he caught it just in time & went around after he had full flaps down. Had he let his wheels down then he would not have gotten out. You cannot go around with full flaps and wheels down on single engine. McBride's brake failed and he did a beautiful job of holding it down and the plane was not damaged — only blew a tire. On a test hop the turbos didn't cut in, later did aerobatics. Everyone is off tomorrow — another Corsair went down at Rabaul. The New Zealand Air Force Squadron is now pulling out from us.

24 June — Played softball this morning and didn't do much the rest of the day.

25 June — . . . We practiced weaving for an hour. This afternoon had a lecture by Major [*Robert B.*] Westbrook — he has fourteen planes to his credit. We enjoyed his lecture very much as he knew what he was talking about. . . .

26 June — Formation and more weaving & gunnery. I led a flight of three this afternoon with my ship being a piggy back. They didn't give me a bucket to take along. The poor guy [*my passenger*] . . . got quite sick. What

Bob Morriss (standing on the left), Bill Gaskill, Junior Cunningham, Sparks, McBride, and others are listening to Colonel Leo F. Dusard and Colonel Robert B. Westbrook, Jr., review a strike.

a mess the cockpit was — and I almost got sick from the smell. We stayed up the full hour & a half, but it was almost torture for both of us. We did loops, rolls & Immelmans. Cunningham stayed right on my wing & Morriss not far behind. The six-thirty flights don't suit me very much — and I am glad we don't get those all of the time. It seems that I am the third highest in the squadron in combat time. Worley & Sun are above me. . . .

Bob Morriss flew as the author's wing man on many missions until he was shot down by shore guns in New Guinea.

An earthquake today which lasted for quite awhile. The volcano is really pouring forth the smoke now.

27 June — Formation again today practicing weaving. I led the flight today — there was plenty of room for improvement. We climbed steadily at 500' per and at an airspeed of 190; however I didn't keep a constant airspeed. Col. [*Leo*] Dusard [*347th Group Commanding Officer*] came up from Stirling today & gave us a good talk. Major Westbrook went back to Stirling. Oh yes, we feathered our engines today — and rolled with a dead engine!! I am getting more & more confidence — at least I am finding more things to do with this plane. I already have all the confidence you could imagine — maybe too much!! But I really wouldn't change ships for anything now!

ABOUT THIS TIME, one day Captain Stege asked Junior Cunningham to take the jeep and go to the flight line for something. Junior said, "But, Sir, I don't know how to drive." Captain Stege spent the rest of the afternoon showing him how to drive a jeep. Junior was one of the best fliers I ever knew, and he had not yet learned to drive a car! In those days, I guess young people from the city just didn't get the chance to learn. But in the rural areas it was different; we drove a truck as soon as we were able to reach the brake and steering wheel at the same time. On the school bus route, near the end, the driver would let one of us kids drive. The insurance companies would shudder today.

This was a debriefing where the leaders are going over the mission and giving suggestions on how the pilots could do better. It must have been a publicity shot, as many cameramen are there.

One day Sergeant Ken Gerhardt, a friend of mine from Willcox, Arizona, told his driver to take the next day's strike papers up the hill for the next day's missions. After a while the soldier came back and said the jeep couldn't climb the hill. The Sergeant was perturbed and went out with the guy and put it in first gear and then second and went up the hill. The guy said, "I didn't know you could shift it with the engine running."

We pilots received a liquor ration of two ounces for each mission. Some of us would pool that, then trade it to some guys to go and catch us a mess of fish, and we would all have a fish fry. Now that was living!

Sometimes we were attached to different outfits for chow and quarters. The Navy fed us really well; and with the Marines it was excellent; but with the Army it was lots of C-rations. With the Australians — well, one day I started for the mess hall, and I could smell it from a long way off. When I got there, I faced a heaping tub of sheep's tongues about one-third or one-half cooked. I couldn't take that, so I went back to my tent. Sometimes, about 10:30 at night, the mess sergeant would cook up a tub of hot chocolate and make toasted cheese sandwiches. That was good.

We were fortunate enough most of the time to have tents with coral sand floors, or sometimes even wood, and cots and air mattresses with mosquito netting over the beds.

In one place we were attached to the Marines and lived in quonset huts.

We flew combat, then came home to shower. We found our beds made and even our shoes shined — figure that out!

One day a plane flew in from Australia with a plane load of fresh eggs, and we had an egg fry. Major Worley got out his trumpet and played "Carnival of Venice." It was the most beautiful sound I ever heard in the jungle.

28 June — Formation & weaving. . . . Morriss had to return — but just as he started home both motors cut out. Dead stick landing!! He was at 23,000' so he coasted all the way home. . . . Received orders to go to Sydney [*Australia, on R&R*]. Hooray! Pack, pack, & pack some more. The other day we were issued air mattresses, new helmets & goggles, etc. Sure is a luxury.

30 June, 10:20 — We are on Scat bound for 'Canal. Four of us. Worley, Cunningham, Morriss & I. The "power flight"! . . . Last night Major Shapiro came in & told us what excellent work we had done etc. this trip and that he was glad that we were going. He was very nice & wished us luck — and a big time!

7 July 1944 — We arrived in Sydney about the 2nd of July. The first place we hit . . . we went straight to a milk bar — soda fountain — and drank all the milk we could hold [*which was dumb because it made me kind of sick.*]. . . Sun's flight arrived yesterday with the report that we had lost three more planes. . . .

8 July — . . . Not a cloud in the sky — however to me it is quite "chilly." I bought a short coat this morning. I still have a bad cold. Last night I rode on my first electric train. . . .

13 July — We are back in Guadalcanal again. . . . Just after we landed another C-47 came in and cracked up. . . . We have learned of two more crack ups in the Sqdn, but still we are lucky that no one was killed — that must make about 9 planes lost in less than a month of checking out [*transition flying*]. The recent ones were [*Lieutenant Lester*] Leidy's prop flew off & then the engine caught fire — the prop hit Ostrander's tail who immediately went into a spin. He saw he didn't have a tail so he bailed out too. Both are okay. . . .

14 July — At last I am back with the Squadron. . . . Major Worley has been transferred to Op. [*Operations*] & is Group Operation officer — more power to him, but his squadron has lost its best man . . . I am proud of him. He talked to me again [*and told me*] how much he appreciated my work, in his flight. . . . After that he and I went to McBee's grave and for the first time I saw him pray. (I did likewise.) He has been like a father to me. I wanted to tell him a few things, but I guess I just wasn't cut out that way. . . .

We are all packed & ready for moving. . . . I won't say where we are going. . . .

17 July — . . . Tokyo Radio continues to inform us of the fabulous numbers of our planes that are shot down. . . . Major Shapiro called me in this afternoon and talked to me. He seemed quite distressed and upset over the morale or friction in the squadron. I felt sorry for him & I don't envy his job a bit. He knew that I had been very close to Major Worley and he was afraid that I might possibly have been bitter or something I suppose. Anyway — he was very nice and complimented my work very highly. . . . The C.O. told me I was given a "Superior" rating by him. . . . [*This made me feel good.*]

19 July — The sqdn — ground echelon — moved out today. There were some duty assignments today and [*Captain*] DeAngelo and I are the two sqdn test pilots. . . .

21 July — Flew for the first time in three weeks and I was over-controlling in tight formation (24 ship). Lt. [*Theodore E.*] Lilly blew a rod on takeoff but he made it okay. . . . I went down early this morning and helped preflight my plane. . . .

22 July — . . . I spent the day going around with Capt Jarrell helping check on the planes, moving etc. . . .

23 July — . . . I used the armament truck to go for the mail and for the men who were working at Piva on the P-38 which landed there. Was also down at the docks watching the efficient loading and unloading of boats and barges. Also watched with great interest the "Ducks" (amphibious six-wheeled vehicles — LC's) as they wallowed along in the enormous waves carrying personnel and cargo to and from the ships.

24 July — . . . I had a test hop & slow time this afternoon late. Went to Piva South strip — took off in the rain. Surely was a swell ship J-20 — cruise at 245 [mph] at 30" — 2450 rpm and exceptionally smooth & quiet. . . . [*Lieutenant Don*] Raymond took off today & his canopy flew off — "head up & locked"! [*When the cause is in question, the accident committee always calls it "pilot error" so that other pilots won't think the plane is dangerous.*]

26 July — . . . [*Lieutenant Sylvester "Joe"*] Owens went in the drink just after he peeled off for a landing. Engines lost power. It is the opinion of the investigating committee etc. etc. "cockpit trouble" [*pilot error*]. That brings our squadron total up to about eleven airplanes (P-38s) in the last six weeks . . . but . . . no pilots have been killed. [*The Japanese might have liked to give us a medal.*]. . . Owens was very lucky to get out without being hurt. A destroyer picked him up. The plane had its wheels part way down & it flipped over on its back. Also this evening I enjoyed hearing the RNZAF [*Royal New Zealand Air Force*] Band — one of the largest bands I have ever seen. . . .

27 July — Help load a truck [*for the move*] . . . most manual labor I have done in a long time. . . . Our mail is not coming thru. I guess it has been forwarded to the rest of the sqdn which has not yet reached their destination. The Japs still have the airfield we are going to land on. . . .

28 July — Had a test hop today that was important — it was to determine the mysterious cause of the accidents we have had in this squadron. It was the most thorough check I could make. The same ship came in on a dead engine this morning so I tried to determine the cause. I spent the full hour & a half making notes etc. of all the instruments on dead & single engine procedure. . . . It all boiled down to the fact there is the element of human error or "cockpit trouble." I guess that will be the verdict until we can get something more definite. . . .

30 July — Two acceptance checks on two J-25's. . . . The first one stepped right on up to 30,000 feet in 20 minutes . . . it trimmed up and flew like a dream. The second one had belly tanks but it still flew swell. [*It could do this in less than half that time but why burn it up on a test hop!*]. . .

1 August 1944 — Flew in sqdn formation today — it surely is a clumsy thing but I guess we will see the value of it in a few days. . . . It is about the safest unit that we can fly. . . . We haven't cracked up any planes lately — I wonder why!!

2 August — Spent the day working on plane & trying to get it ready to go. The carburetor had been faulty — have another on now, but there are several things yet to fix on it. Need a new fuel pressure gauge. This ship has given considerable trouble on the left engine. Heard the presidential speech of the new president of the Philippines. Will go in a few minutes to hear a band concert. Bob Hope & F[*rances*] Langford are giving a performance on the island tonight.

3 August — This morning we went to a lecture on jungle survival. This afternoon we went with two Australian officers and a native out into the "bush" as they call it and they showed us the different edible foods growing wild in the jungle. Watervines — they literally poured out water when we cut them. Garlic nuts were almost good. Breadfruit trees, banana trees — papaya and a lot of others on which one could, if absolutely necessary, survive for awhile.

4 August — Flew 116 today and it did all right. Poor landing though and everyone was watching me too. . . .

5 August — Sqdn formation again today . . . (24 planes) formed up on course in 15 minutes. I think we landed in 13 minutes. . . . Willie [*Lieutenant William G.*] Keyworth [*Jr.*] forgot and pushed his bomb release instead of the mike button & dropped both belly tanks in the bay!! He and Junior worked hard getting two new tanks fitted on. . . . Lt. [*Jerome A. "Mike"*] Mikylvedt and I are assigned the same plane — #100. I spent the afternoon cleaning and polishing it. It is a P-38J-15LO. It was the one I stepped right on up to 30,000 on a test-acceptance check the other day.

6 August — Spent the morning cleaning my [*pistol*] & other equipment. . . . It rained off and on all day.

7 August — Still nothing new. 339th & 67th flew up today. . . .

8 August — Spent the morning cleaning the "shark's teeth" off the plane and scraping off the glue. It really is a job. . . .

9 August — . . . Tonight I had a bad touch of homesickness — the inactivity is getting not a little [*tiresome*]. I felt like praying for some reason or another so I did. I guess I should go to church sometime — maybe it will help out. Last night was another earthquake — at 02:00 this morning rather. There will be another one tonight.

11 August — Earthquake again this morning — it is almost getting to be a habit. . . . Capt Jarrell got bitten by a centipede — it put him in bed for all day. There are a lot of insects and things here, but not too bad though.

13 August — This is it! (in meeting tonight) happy landings.

14 August — "Dry run"! maybe tomorrow.

<u>15 August</u> — We left today and arrived in the Admiralties (550 mi.). It is nice here. The two airstrips are about the longest I have seen and are of coral. The coral is terribly hard on the eyes & the sun and glare is terrific — the evenings are cool & nice though. There are a lot of planes here from the 5th, 13th, and 7th air forces. . . .

16 August — We didn't leave — nor will we leave for quite a few days — spent the day talking with Australian pilots. . . .

17 August — Last night we were given sudden notice to pick up — we spent the night loading the planes. . . . Left early this morning. Am on the plane now — fighter escort. The weather has been lousy all the way. Later — we landed. MIDDLEBURG ISLAND

18 August — This is a tiny islet [*four miles from Cape Sansapor, northwest coast of New Guinea*] with 52 hundred [*foot*] strip running full length

The 240-acre coral Middleburg Island off the northwest coast of New Guinea, where the author spent six months. The airstrip is overlaid with steel landing mat.

— excellent strip of coral & steel matting. . . . This is a beehive of activity. . . . There is dense jungle and marshes here with cocoanut trees. We are expecting an air raid any minute. Now that there are so many planes here — Tokyo Rose said they would be here to greet us. . . . we are on the very front lines!! We surely did get our foxholes dug in. . . .

The weather is bad but it is quite sandy here. . . . The place is loaded with typhus and malaria . . . the rest of the Sqdn is on the mainland of New Guinea, Cape Sansapor which is a tiny filthy perimeter. . . . Our strip is partly submerged at high tide. Boy what a place!!! . . . We are covered with clothes and insect repellant & sweat & didn't shave lately. Surely appreciate my air mattress now! We have to set up our own tents etc. We have a portable trailer of food — the chow they serve is good — tastes good after working so hard although it is only C-rations. Of course there is a shortage of drinking water & of course no water to bathe in. . . . We have to sleep under mosquito bars — No lights — no biscuit gun in the tower — let alone a radio. Army engineers are on this place & are really efficient. . . . Bulldozers run most of the night but you won't see us staying awake at night from the noise as we are too tired . . .

20-21-22 August — . . . Yesterday I stood scramble alert. This morning we stood scramble alert again & flew dawn patrol. . . . We looked over the island — the orbit points etc. Golly, of all the code names we have to learn,

-17 August Note. Moved to Middleburg Island - N.G.

DATE 19	AIRCRAFT IDENT. MARK	MAKE - MODEL AND HORSEPOWER OF AIRCRAFT	FROM	TO	CLASS OR TYPE			DURATION OF FLIGHT Total Time to Date
			Middleburg I.				T. this month	757:20
22 August	P38 J-15 -	ALLISON E.	Local					759:10
25 "	2	1420 H.P.	"	"				760:30
27 "	1718-89-91							764:50
29 "	"		Namelo	"				768:00
31 "	"	"	Samate	"			21:50	772:55
1 Sept	"	"	Local					773:40
3 "	"	"	" Samate Joffman					775:20
4 "	"	"	Middleburg -	Local				777:20
5 "	"	"	Middleburg - Celebes -	Local				783:00
7 "	"	"	" Namelo	"				786:55
11 "	"	"	Boroe + Ceram	" "				791:00
16 "	"	"	Middleburg -	Local				793:15
18 "	"	"	"	"				794:20
19 "	"	"	"	"				797:05
			CARRY TOTALS FORWARD TO TOP OF NEXT PAGE					

On 17 August 1944 the author's Pilot Log notes that he had moved to Middleburg Island, New Guinea, area: "We are now with the 13th Air Task Force, 68th Fighter Squadron."

ea area. We are now 13th Air Task Force - 68th Ftr Sqdn

~~SOLO FLIGHT TIME~~ Combat Total/ ~~Day~~ Combat	~~Night~~	~~Instrument~~	~~LINK~~	DUAL INSTRUCTION	as Instructor or Student		REMARKS: Each maneuver and the time spent thereon, attested to by the Instructor is to be entered in this column for all instruction received. Any serious damage to the aircraft MUST be entered here also.
245:15	Escort	DB+S.	Patrol	RSA.	Test.		
247			1:45				Dawn Patrol [illegible]
248:20				120			[illegible] 1 flight [illegible]
		4:20					Strafe [illegible]
256:40		4:00					DB + strafe " " (AA)
261:35		2:15	1:40		1:00		[illegible] (AA)
262:20					0:45		112 - good [illegible]
264:00		1:40					[illegible]
266:00				2:00			scramble - 2 planes shot down - 67th. pilot
271:40	5:40						B 24s - saw one "oscar" 2 others [illegible]
275:35		3:55					[illegible] good hit [illegible]
279:40		4:05					" " Ambon [illegible]
281:55	2:15						Aborted mission - due weather
28[illegible]					1:00		#111 - 50 Gas fumes - J.K. Acrobatics
285:45	2:45						Task [illegible]
							PILOT'S SIGNATURE

Dancer Blue Flight: (from left to right) Alfred P. Ostrander, Lester R. Leidy, Charles A. "Pappy" Pearce, Richard D. Wilkinson; Dancer Red Flight: (from center to right) Captain John Stege (CO), Edwin R. ("Junior") Cunningham, Bill Gaskill, Bob Morriss.

also code names on the grid maps . . . soon we will have electric lights I hope. The candle chandelier hanging from the mosquito net overhead is definitely cute. The floor is of clean coral sand — there are several tents joined together with trench foxholes in between. . . .

23 August — We were busy today. I went over to the mainland and got my B-4 bag & footlocker. [*Another squadron*] came up today & their formation was a screwed up affair & their landings were awful — never again will I complain about my landings. . . . Heard that 77 B-29s made another raid on Japan. Hooray!! However they lost four. [*They were way north of us.*]. . .

24 August — Went over to mainland today. Sqdn had first big mission — it didn't pan out as we didn't meet the B-25s at rendezvous. Better luck next time. All is well otherwise.

25 August — This evening Lt. Gerald D. Kelly came in from dusk patrol. (we don't know why he came in early) He undershot and hit his left wheel on the bank or hump on the end of the runway, shearing off the left l[*anding*] gear. He dropped his left wing & plowed off to the left into the 339th airplanes parked beside the runway. It exploded and burned instantly. He never had a chance. He was a swell fellow and he was very soon to go home. He was lately talking about it and the wedding he was going to have in the church. He was quite sick today and hasn't been feeling well for the last few days. The fire & explosion was enormous & ammunition and gas tanks & planes blew up & burned fiercely for 20 minutes. It is still burning. Luckily, as far as we know, only one Enlisted man [*on the ground*] was injured — he had been knocked out of the cockpit of one of the parked planes. Four new P-38s from the 339th Sqdn and of course the one of ours was destroyed. Also a weapons carrier & 2 jeeps completely destroyed. There was an emergency landing immediately after the accident but that pilot and plane got down okay (barely).

This morning I flew on a scramble — it was a horrible exhibition of flying on my part, which was due to the poor attitude I have had lately. . . .

We are all quite sad at the loss of our buddy. . . . A P-40 (RAAF [*Royal Australian Air Force*] pilot) crashed & burned on the strip. The pilot had gas fumes in the cockpit & passed out just as he came in and leveled off.

Luckily the pilot got out without being killed. He was still doped up but he was cleared up enough to get out of the plane before it went up in flames. He suffered concussion and shock and other injuries.

Soon (tomorrow maybe) we are scheduled to go to the Halmaheras on a long mission. I hope we have good luck.

I am going to close this diary tonight with this quotation from Joshua 1:9 which Mother wrote in my little testament — "Be strong and of good courage: be not afraid, neither be thou dismayed for the Lord thy God is with thee whithersoever thou goest."

God bless Lt. Kelly and his beloved ones who will be grieved. God bless my mother and father and wife and brothers and their families. May this war end soon with a minimum of lives lost, and then may we all return to our homes & live in peace and happiness. AMEN. Air Raid. I hate it in the foxholes!

27 August — Red alert at 0200 but no bombs were dropped. Went on a mission this afternoon. . . . On the way back we flew over Sarong — one of the hottest spots down in the SWPA. They threw so much stuff up at us that it was a wonder we weren't all hit. . . .

28 August — Several alerts last night. . . . Three more P-38s were destroyed on the ground. . . . Why can't we take off?? We could get them [*the enemy*] I am sure. Ftr command says no. Three other planes were damaged including the P-61 of General Barnes. Incidentally the P-61 hasn't been worth its salt yet! It isn't entirely their fault however, as the mountains, weather, etc. really screws up their radar.

This is a very small island — 5400 ft long & about as wide. Anywhere a bomb hits damage will be heavy. Two men killed and sixteen injured last night. Now the 67th has arrived — more planes, less room — greater fire hazards. . . .

29 August — Spent night on mainland & watched air show on the little island. More damage done! Went to Namlea [*port on Buru Island, west of Ceram*] — 4 hours again.

30 August — Today I talked with Major Shapiro and told him of all my troubles. He was very sympathetic & gave me much encouragement. . . .

31 August — . . . Fred Belue cracked up again: the worst looking wreck I have ever seen where the pilot walked away without a scratch. He had been shot up pretty bad, no brakes, no hydraulic system, no nothing.

1 September 1994 — Test hop. One photo ship & pilot crashed in the drink on take off. Too bad — they are doing a swell job.

2 September — 1 hr. 40 min. mission on one of the best yet. Morriss [*my wing man*] got a "Dinah" [*Jap plane*] on the ground at Jeffman isle. We strafed personnel and trucks on runway at Samate. I knocked out two gun positions — 1 h[*eavy*] & 1 light, and Morriss and I together destroyed a third. We made three passes on the target. I was hit by a 6mm slug in the bulkhead just forward of the left coolant radiator (out for repairs!). It was surely a surprise attack & little Japs ran & scattered but they fell like flies. We hedgehopped (after gaining terrific speed) out of the clouds & onto the deck. We came over the end of the runway & caught everything by surprise. Ten B25s went out on a mission. 4 were shot down, three damaged and had to land here. A 90mm coastal gun fired right through between my booms. Another FotoJo hit the drink when forced to do the impossible — go around on one engine, wheels & flaps down. Pilot okay! The first fighter escort to Philippines yesterday — 5th Air Force staging thru here. . . .

ON THE LAST PASS OF THIS MISSION, Morriss yelled on his radio "move over" and he changed course enough to fire on a hangar with a plane in it. It all blew and burned but I had to pull up very sharply in order to miss a clump of coconut palms. As I did, the most awful explosion I ever heard in my life went off, deafening me, and blinding me for just an instant. I barely was able to recover. Then we tore out toward the sea and then home. What I didn't know was that there was a large coastal gun in that camouflaged area. The gunner fired dead on but the missile went right between my booms and at the trailing edge of my cockpit. Any ordinary airplane would have been blasted out of the sky, but due to the twin-boom configuration of this plane the missile went through the middle without touching anything. My Engineering Officer wanted me to explain how I got powder burns underneath both booms and through the trailing edge of the cockpit. That was a close call! Several small-arms-fire bullets also hit the plane but did no damage.

4 September — Scheduled for Celebes strike, mission cancelled. Tide has come in & practically submerged us! We were scrambled when two planes were shot down at Jeffman & Samate. Capt. Hicks went in — but Springer got out — at first it was Lt. Jewell who went in, but turned out to be mistake — it was his flight leader instead. . . .

5 September — Longest mission yet! to Celebes — Langoan A/D escorting Boxcars. Saw three "Oscars," but they were well on their way away from there with the 5th AAF boys in hot pursuit. They lost them in clouds! The mission was 5:40 minutes. . . .

6 September — Had a tooth pulled today. . . . Our Sqdn had its first mission to the Philippines — how I did want to go. . . .

11 September — Another good mission — Namlea & Ceram — Strafed & set fire to a radio station & buildings — three "Sugar Charlies" [*our code names for Japanese small boats*] were destroyed or damaged. We really had a good time. The boats were duck soup. They were heading for shore but didn't make it!. . . 4:05 — plenty of gas left.

Morriss just received word of his father's death. What a blow to him.

12 September — Another day on mainland — trouble in my tooth — had to operate & put a stitch in it. . . . Last night searchlights were turned on for a pilot — 67th boy MIA. This morning Lt. Shevak took off & crashed in the drink, exploded & burned — KIA. He was also of 67th & a very good friend of Harvey, Mills & Worley & that bunch. A very mysterious accident. 339th also lost a good man off of Westbrook's wing, KIA.

14 September — Have returned to Middleburg — another 67th pilot hit the drink. He is okay.

15 September — . . . Lt. Troupe of 67th Sqdn. was shot down at Boroe. He must have been injured as he pulled up — stalled, spun, half recovered — then went in and exploded. He was of the same bunch that came over with Morriss, Cunningham, Keyworth, . . . That brings our losses (347th Ftr group) up to seven since arriving on this island — Middleburg!! on the 17th of last month. 67th lost 4, 68th lost 1, 339th lost 2. . . .

16 September — Today another thing happened when the flight leader tried to climb over a large cumulus cloud — he stalled his whole flight out in the cloud. Everyone was scattered from "Hell to breakfast" & so the whole Squadron had to return. . . . I was terribly afraid . . . Junior in & we spent a half hour hunting for him. He was okay! Once again we have stuck our necks out unnecessarily. . . .

19 September — Task Force cover but couldn't find the task force — hunted for 2 hours. "So solly one of our task forces missing"! 18th group plane overshot runway today, pilot okay though. . . . Still no mail.

20 September — Yesterday's count — 12th Ftr Sqdn 18th Group lost 4 planes & 2 pilots — weather & crash landings. . . .

21 September — Best flight I have had in a long time. All other flights turned back because of the weather but we went around & thru it & to the target in the Celebes. We were to escort CAT [*PBY*] but he also turned back so we just went on for what we could find to strafe. We found a large Jap transport which we decided to strafe — but no results observed & believe transport was already out of commission. . . . We looked over the airdromes: tried to scare up something but couldn't. . . . Mission was 5:40 [*5 hours, 40 minutes*]. . . .

22 September — Lt. Spiller got lost today from Col. Westbrook & Stege's flight was scrambled to search. We later heard that he crash landed. . . . The weather had closed in here — we got down okay I guess, although controller kept telling us to go to Noemfoor [*off the northwest coast of New Guinea*]. I skidded down the runway & ruined two tires — it was very slick & I went all over the place before I managed to stop — What weather!!

24 September — Kendari cancelled again. One replacement today. Lt. Fredrick A. Roos [*my friend*].

25 September — To Kendari. B-24 Escort. 11 of us got to target. Col. Dusard leading, Cunningham on his wing. I [*was*] element [*leader*] & Morriss on my wing. Four Hamps [*Japanese fighter planes*] jumped us from the rear. Did a 180 and met them. They broke up. Our flight stayed up while others went down after the Japs. Another lone Hamp sneaked up behind the four of us. We whipped around. Junior got lost & yelled "get that so and so off my tail." I didn't see Junior any more for awhile. Nip broke off, half rolled & down. We went to the deck where that Jap put on the most superb exhibition of flying I have ever seen. He made us with our old trucks look like bulls in a china closet — the way he maneuvered. He would half roll on the deck — split "S" at 3,000 feet . . . he would whip in and out of our sights. . . . The other boys came over & joined us & it was a merry rat race. . . . On one 360 I met him head on at 30 degree deflection — saw [*my*] cannon shell explode in his left wing — so did Col. Dusard & Col. Westbrook. They picked him up & everyone I do believe got in a burst at him before Col. Westbrook slipped in and finished him off. His wing came off & he quarter rolled, hit the trees & ground, exploded & burned. We had him all boxed off & Westy had a no-deflection shot. . . . In the meantime Raymond & Bryant & Sparks all got after another which went down & crashed. The bombers did a good job to!! The mission was 6:55 [*6 hours, 55 minutes*]. . . .

28 September — Fighter sweep to Halmaheras: D.B. boats etc. Morriss came all the way home on one engine & made a *good* landing. Dooly 1st, Willie, Sun, & Kelly Captains!

29 September — . . . Mail service okay now.

30 September — T.F. [*Task Force*] cover again — 5 hours. Were alerted for hurricane but didn't reach here. . . .

1 October 1944 — Air raid last night, 2 officers & one man were killed on mainland.

2 October — Another TF cover.

3 October — Morriss & I took off to look for Lt. Salling who was shot down at Ceram. He was okay & was picked up by Dumbo. B-24s got it again when they went to Borneo and nearly 30% out of 72 were lost! That is really rough. Golly how I feel sorry for those fellows. Soon we will be going there from [*refueling in*] Morotai I guess. How I am ready to go!

4 October — Our fellows went to Halmahera. Lt. Richard B. O'Mara killed. He dived straight into the ground at terrific speed. One of the nicest fellows in the Sqdn. We don't understand why either. He had such a terrific speed at such a low altitude in a vertical dive that I guess he just couldn't recover. [*Maybe compressibility*] How we do feel bad about it. I have flown with him several times. A good flyer and a credit to any man's army. We lost a valuable man. . . .

5 October — . . . Spiller just came in — a nice gesture on his part that he is accepting a small donation — for Lt. O'Mara's church to get something in memory of him.

7 October — Scramble alert this afternoon — to sink a downed P-40. [*We never did find it.*] We landed long after dark. Climbed up to 11,000 ft coming across the mountains and clouds and after awhile I contacted auto crystal and got homing — I was exactly on course so we came on in. It was very dark — Morriss made three passes at the field. Keyworth went off in ditch. Cunningham ran over a bank. Morriss stopped until someone came after him with lights. I got by okay though. Cunningham's ship may have to be salvaged. The mission was negative because of limited time and weather.

Later: Hooray — Cunningham's plane will be saved.

8 October — . . . Some guy bailed out of a P-38 today — he was a full Col. and a command pilot. I guess he got "buck fever" or something!! . . .

9 October — Four of us were scrambled at noon today as several planes and fighters landed at Namlea today. . . . as it was we destroyed four on the ground & damaged a fourth. A very good mission for a change. No mail tonight.

10 October — We evacuated the strip [*because of a hurricane warning*]

— 18 airplanes from our Sqdn & likewise from the other two in the Group. We went all the way down to Wadke to RON (remain overnight). Of all the awful "dumps" that is the worst I have been to yet!! Small island. No shade — very dusty or muddy or both. However it is a good strip.

12 October — Ten men were killed today when a B-25 cut out on takeoff with full bomb and gas load. The crew was okay because they fled from the scene, only the curious bystanders were victims! Also four P-38s were ditched in formation near Salawati: They were lost — 44th Sqdn!!

13 October — Flew dusk patrol tonight — otherwise all has been quiet. Ostrander and Sparks flew with Morriss and me.

14 October and 15 October — We went to Noemfoor (200 mi) RON at the 307th Bomb Group. They were nice fellows — they have had it pretty rough too. We returned this morning. I led the group (347th group) however only 18 of us went. . . .

16 October — Good mission to Laboeha — the best dive bomb mission that I have been on — in this P-38. Beautiful target and we each carried 2 - 500# bombs & on our dive bomb run & everything was excellent. . . . Many buildings were destroyed — we (our flight) started a very large fire.

17 October — . . . Long mission to Borneo again tomorrow and again I don't get to go. I wish I could instead of going on rest leave (which I was supposed to go on — today). Now the rest leave is postponed until the 20th.

18 October — Test hop today. . . . I pulled up beside a [*British fighter bomber*] beaufighter — one of their chaps pulled up a large camera and took my picture. He . . . sent me the negative. The mission to Borneo fizzled out. Lt. Love went in the drink in 115. He was okay though. . . . I saved 2 P-40s today when one had a slight accident on the runway. I ran down the embankment waving my shirt [*and threw it in the air*] and out on the runway and the P-40 behind Snafu [*situation normal all fouled up*] saw me and swerved & narrowly missed Snafu. It surely was close. The visibility in the 40 is so very bad on landing that I guess it has had more

Bill Gaskill on Middleburg Island, New Guinea.

Bill Gaskill on a test hop, 18 October 1944. New Guinea is in the background.

landing accidents than about any other fighter. I would guess that the P-39 has had about the least no. of [*landing*] accidents.

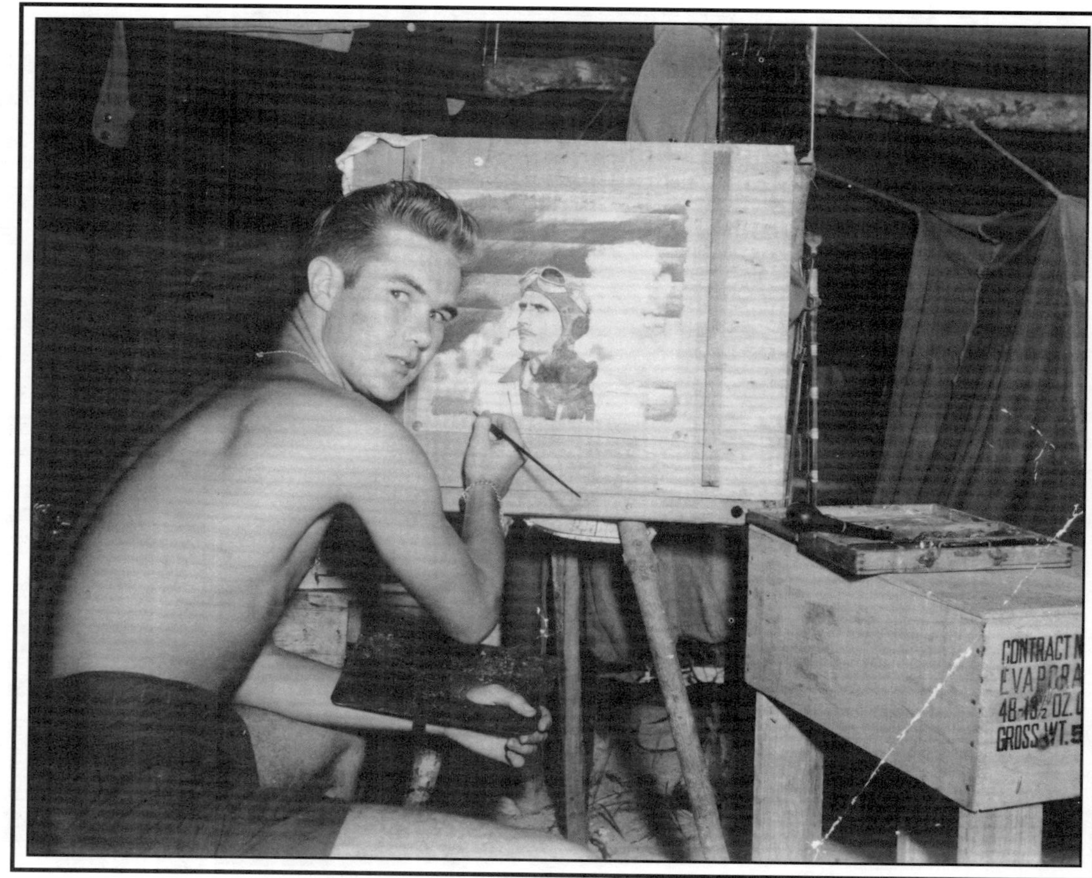

"Junior" (Lieutenant Edwin R.) Cunningham drawing Colonel Robert B. Westbrook, Jr. He was as good an artist as he was a flier.

Bill Gaskill's friend, Fred Roos — an excellent pilot.

Junior Cunningham drew this picture of himself and Lieutenant William M. Gaskill (Willie) of Dancer Red Flight, 68th Fighter Squadron, 347th Group, 13th Air Force, sitting under Cunningham's plane (#112). The author's plane, #100, was nearby in the picture. The men were standing "scramble alert" in the South Pacific awaiting the siren for them to take off after "bogies" (the enemy). Cunningham and Gaskill flew many missions together in both P-39 and P-38 aircraft. Cunningham was an excellent artist, an outstanding pilot, a "great wing man," and a very good friend.

3 November 1944 — I have just returned from a swell rest leave (10 days) in Sydney. . . . to find that the Japs are giving the boys of Leyte a bad time of it. Incidentally since my last entry there have been many important battles with the Japs. Including the landing in the Philippines. Good deal!!!! [*MacArthur has returned!!*] I also found out that Major Worley got a Jap plane to his credit! . . .

6 November — Longest mission yet, 10 hrs & 15 min. to the Philippines — we missed the fight though. . . . The Fifth Air Force had a good time though — we flew all around . . . trying to stir up something but they wouldn't come up & fight. . . . We landed & refueled both ways at Morotai. . . . We are afraid to go in to Leyte as they are too trigger happy. One P-38 took off there & some joker [*one of our own gunners*] shot out his engine so he made an attempt to emergency land on the other engine with wheels and flaps down — they shot out his other engine [*This was friendly fire.*] — he went in the drink. . . . I hardly feel like protecting someone as ignorant or careless as all that. They have shot down many of our own planes, including 2 PBYs no less. . . .

9 November — Flew co-pilot in B-24 today. . . . [*I was actually co-pilot in name only because I really didn't know anything about flying it.*]

10 November — Had my finger operated on today — also took Typhus & Cholera shots. . . .

11 November — Test hop & slow time. I buzzed the field on single engine which caused considerable excitement. Capt. Scott (67th) & Lt. Shaw went down on Kendari mission.

12 November — Capt. Scott & Lt. Shaw were both picked up. . . . "Red" Garrison was killed when he tried to go around on one engine. I received the news from his mother in a letter today.

14 November — Awakened at 04:15 — ate breakfast then flew dawn patrol. It was beautiful this morning — the clouds were all colors just before sunrise & we did acrobatics & had a good rat race. Later Sparks & I flew a tracking mission [*to give practice to radar men on the ground to track aircraft*]. We are having good breakfasts now — two eggs (fried) plus sausage meat or Spam, coffee & toast. Everything rather quiet — nothing much doing.

15 November — . . . No mail for several days — I believe that our mail went down with a C-47 recently — golly I hate to think of that — how petty that sounds!! When there are lives lost I worry about mail. . . .

18 November — To Borneo — Tarakan . . . 347th group in a coordinated attack on Tarakan to hit oil tanks, ship yards and gun positions. It was a complicated plan . . . .

ON 18 NOVEMBER 1944, a big mission was scheduled to fly from Middleburg Island to Tarakan, a small island off the coast of Borneo, to strafe and bomb the rich oil fields and gun installations there. The 347th Fighter Group scheduled 26 P-38s for this mission.

On our P-38s we carried 400 gallons of gas plus a 300-gallon belly tank of extra fuel, also a bomb and a full load of 50-caliber and 20mm ammunition. We had four 50-caliber machine-guns and one 20mm cannon. This was very formidable firepower for that time: it was sure death to small boats and anything else that got in the way.

The pilots wore a parachute, a rubber inflatable boat, a jungle pack, and a Mae West, all strapped on all the time we were in the plane. The jungle pack contained a large machete, a flare pistol, and a money pouch containing gold and silver coins and Dutch paper money. Also there was a first-aid kit and a 45-caliber pistol. How you could get out of a drowning plane with all of that on in just a matter of seconds is a minor miracle.

Our ground crew did an excellent job of keeping our planes airworthy. They deserve a great deal of the credit for the work they did that contributed to our successes.

We were to fly from Middleburg Island to Morotai, fuel up and continue to target, return to Morotai, refuel and return home. It was a long mission — 300 miles from Middleburg to Morotai, plus 748 more miles past and return. The sortie was about 9 hours, but over the next five days I flew over 30 hours to complete this particular mission.

My wing man for that particular day was Lieutenant Sylvester "Joe" Owens, but he couldn't take off for some reason. Later he did take off and tried to catch us. Colonel Dusard, I think it was, told him to go back if he didn't see us in the next five minutes, after which time there would be strict radio silence. Owens either didn't hear or else disregarded the order. The last 200 miles to the target we flew very low to escape radar detection. We encountered no enemy air resistance.

As we approached the target, all hell broke loose. Another squadron heard the distress call from Lieutenant Owens. "I am hit — my face is bloody, I am going in. . . ." What happened was that he was the last one to the target, and all remaining Japanese guns were trained on him. I had a hung bomb (the electric solenoid couldn't release it). I finally managed to manually release it, but had I been able to have dropped it on my assigned target (an antiaircraft nest) Owens might not have been shot down; who knows? Owens managed to turn back to sea. He lost altitude and water landed, got out of the plane quickly and into his inflatable raft, and then passed out. I hadn't heard any of that because I had needed all of the electric energy to try to work the solenoid, so I had turned off my radio for a time.

I fired my guns at a nondescript looking hut, and it exploded to smithereens. The hut must have contained ammunition. I successfully avoided hitting the debris from the explosion. We also strafed and bombed oil tanks. When we left the target, the smoke was at 17,000 feet.

As we left the island, there were small transport boats trying to get to port. Our flight, which by then had only three planes, strafed them and set them all on fire. Cunningham dropped down and went after one boat. I almost overshot him, and I chopped my throttles and socked down flaps. We strafed in close formation. Stege and Cunningham were really strafing ahead of me. We made several passes. When we left, there were three bright balls of fire on the water. About 30 miles away, I looked around to see great columns of smoke on the horizon from the oil fields.

Sometime later at the debriefing I asked Junior Cunningham why he was missing his targeted boats; I had seen the ricochets out across the water. He replied with glee, "Couldn't you see all those little heads bobbing in the water?" I guess he just needed a little target practice. On this mission, the Group destroyed or set fire to numerous oil tanks, a tanker, three merchant vessels, nine or ten barges and small boats, and a pumping installation — a large success!

Back to Lieutenant Owens. I felt responsible for my wing man and sought a way to rescue him. I got permission from Colonel Dusard and Major Worley to go back and search for him. I then went to Colonel Ford of the Air Sea Rescue Squadron at Morotai. What a great outfit they were. I explained that we had a man down near Borneo and asked if they would look for him. They told me that if I'd find him, and be there to cover them, they'd pick him up if they were in the area. They showed me a large map with pins in it and said, "We have 60 crews out there to pick up." The Rescue Squadron was flying PBY Catalina flying-boats. To search for a downed pilot 1,050 miles from home was an awfully long way when we weren't even sure he was still afloat.

Lieutenant Morriss, my regular wing man, and I finally got underway and flew to Borneo. We were searching the shoreline when all of a sudden Owens fired his flare pistol in the air! You talk about excited — I was that! I sent Morriss "upstairs" to report in and ask for help, but it was too late in the day for them to come. In the meantime, I wrote a note, put it in my canteen, and threw it in the water. Little native kids swam out and got it. In the note I told him we would be back to pick him up.

Then I spotted a beautiful little coral reef right on the edge of the coast. I said to myself, "I could just land there and pick him up and bring him home piggy back." So I released my 300-gallon belly tank. Well, the darned thing flipped and hit and dented my horizontal stabilizer, which caused buffeting and instability. I was disgusted. I couldn't get slow enough without feeling a peculiar stall characteristic, but that turned out to be lucky for me — what I had thought was a beautiful place to land, Owens later told me, was several feet under the water. It had looked so shallow and clear! Anyway, I chickened out on that deal and joined up with my wing man and proceeded home. I didn't have much more trouble with my airplane as long as I was careful. I reported in to my outfit and to Colonel Ford. To my delight, Colonel Ford said he would have someone available to pick up Owens if we would rendezvous with him over Horseshoe Island just off the northeast coast of Borneo the next morning, 22 November.

I changed planes, and the next morning Lieutenant Everett Magor and I took off. About half way to the target, a large weather front moved in. We almost stalled out trying to climb out through it, and finally we had to be on instruments. My wing man was tucked in real close. Finally we broke out of the weather, and there ahead was Horseshoe Island —

well, not really; I had drifted off course quite a ways. But by the time we had let down, there was "Playmate 22," code name of our PBY Catalina angel of mercy. We proceeded to the area, and sure enough, there was Owens with the natives on the beach. They were dressed in white. The float plane let down and landed while we circled overhead. We knew the Japanese were nearby. The natives rowed Owens out to the plane in a boat. He boarded, and the PBY took off to pick up somebody else from another outfit.

As Owens later related to me, he came to and rowed over to the shore of Borneo. He lay on the beach for a while. He was not injured very badly. He awoke to see some natives coming down the beach. He drew his gun, but realized they were probably friendly. He drew out his money pouch and offered them some. They took him into a village; a native there had athlete's foot. Lieutenant Owens treated the man with ointment from his first-aid kit. The chief of the village got Owens a hut. The next morning, he looked out, and there were natives lined up for sick call! All appeared to have athlete's foot, but one indicated that he was sick to his stomach. Owens was stumped. He got in his medicine pack and gave the man an Atabrine pill (a medication only for malaria). The guy took it, rubbed his stomach, and smiled. He thought he was cured. Word got around! The chief brought Lieutenant Owens a woman to be his housekeeper. Owens went on to tell me that he thought he was set up for the duration! But, no, we had to ruin it!

My wing man and I then climbed way up to go home, and I looked below. There was a big Japanese gunboat coming. I said, "We'll get that guy," and reached over to jettison my nearly empty belly tank. Instead, I jettisoned the full tank. I realized what I had done when the plane lurched up more than it should have. I then released my full tank, leaving only the internal tanks. I didn't have enough fuel to dive down, get that gunboat, regain my altitude, and get home. I didn't know whether my wing man was relieved or disgusted, as I'm sure the gunboat was heavily armed.

As we headed home, we once again encountered the storm front, but it was by then just cloudy, not turbulent. We couldn't climb over it again, so we went on instruments for a long time. I began to sweat my fuel supply. I used every trick in the book to conserve fuel, and somehow we made it to Morotai. We fueled up and then flew on to home base. It was on our way home to Middleburg that I heard about our most respected Executive Officer, Colonel Westbrook, getting shot down while on another mission straf-

220

the enemy. The next thing we
heard was an excited high
pitched voice. "Dancer" - 4
- I am hit - my face is bloody
I am going in - heading 120°
That was all. Up to that time
no one had any knowledge our
even hearing Dancer 4. Some
one sighted him and circled
while Major England climbed
up to get call "Daylight." No
contact. Later Daylight picked
up someone in the drink but
it wasn't Owens. We are
afraid there is no more hope.
Smoke was from 5 or up to
17,000 feet! - Good hunting
- we spent the night in Mortai -
the trip was - 300 miles to "
748 miles to Tarakan 6 hrs 9:05 minutes
19 November
Returned today

23 November
The last few days have been
very strenuous. I took matters
into my own hands - went
to see MAJOR WORLEY

The author's Field Book entry for events of 23 November when they found Lieutenant Joe Owens.

(2 C) Then procured a 67th pl
Then Col. DuSARD. They
thought it was A Good Idea that
I go to AIR FORCE + take
a personal interest in Finding
Joe owens. This I did. I went
to morotai From there got
a clearance to go on A Search
mission. - Capt. Love - Lt. MAGOR
Lt. GASKill + Lt. MORRISS we took off
+ went to TARAKAN. we searched
a long time. I dropped my
300 gal Belly TANK. + hit my
HORIZONTAL Stabilizer + Elevator
causing some buffeting + much of a
drag we searched the coast of
Borneo (750 miles west of
MoroTai). we combed the area
well. Then All of a sudden I
saw a string of smoke. I tore
over there found LT OWENS
I was so happy that I screamed
over the radio for the rest
of the fellows. I circled him
while Morriss went upstairs
to try to contact ("playmate 22")
a rescue plane. He had already return
home. I dropped my

(22) I attempted to land there & pick him up.
-but couldn't set it down.
jungle kit & a note to Owens.
He was jumping up & down
& waving a flag - little native kids
were doing the same. I
circled for a long time then
we had to return to Morotai
as it was getting late & we
~~were~~ couldn't contact any help.
I then went to see Col.
Ford C.O. of the EMERGENCY
Rescue Sqn. He was very glad
to hear of the good news.
He scheduled a Catalina to
go up to get Joe on the
following day. Lt. Magor & I
Rendezvoused with the "cat" next
morning (22 of November) & we escorted
CAT to pick up Joe. The natives
rowed him out to the plane.
I flew over 19 hrs since I left
here the other day. The
weather was bad in places &
& were on instruments
occasionally. On the way
home I landed at Morotai. The
67th ship I was flying was
grounded & they wouldn't let me

223

take off with it. I took Capt Loves ship & came home. Three of our flight are still in Morotai – ships are out.

Lt. Willis Kannikd was MIA (POW?) shot down yesterday at MAKASSAR

Col. Westbrook MIA KIA was shot down also Lt Shrader ok now lost a boy there.

Lt. Stephen A. "Tiger" Born KIA shot down strafing a destroyer.

The 18th group has lost very heavily lately too.

I hope things slack off a bit soon.

(p.s. I was put in for D.F.C.)

24 November

Test Hop Today & had a lot of fun!! Cunningham

25 November

Big party – Grand sendoff for Worley – he is on his way home. Major Wortham too!!

note: Lt. Col. Robert B. Westbrook – one of the finest men we have ever met – 20 planes to his credit to say nothing of all the other damage he has done ... strafing & D.B. ...

ing a Japanese gunboat. I was very sad about that, because our P-38 Lockheed Lightnings excelled on this mission and other long-range missions.

During the period between 18 and 23 November, the mission to Tarakan, we also lost Lieutenant William Kanuika at Makassar [*Strait, between Borneo and the Celibes Islands, off northwest New Guinea*] and Lieutenant Stephen "Tiger" Borne. The 18th Group lost heavily.

25 November — Big party — Grand sendoff for Worley — he is on his way home. Major Wortham too!!
Note: Lt. Col. Robert B. Westbrook [*shot down*] — one of the finest men we have ever met — 20 planes to his credit, to say nothing of all the other damage he has done on strafing and DB missions.

26 November — Received orders dated 11-25-44 — Now I am Flight leader, but will probably fly with my regular flight leader for awhile yet. . . . Am now restricted to not more than 60 hrs per month. . . . Raids on Morotai have been pretty severe. . . . They (Japs) got twenty planes on the ground one night. . . . In Bougainville we use to get three & four missions per day — but they were short. Here we fly one mission every two or three days but they are long. . . .

27 November — Today was just another day which was "negative." (1) Breakfast. (2) down to the [*flight*] line. (3) over to the 11th airdrome to see how they were coming along on P-40 (4) back to the sack. (5) Lunch (sandwich of toasted cheese) (5) back to the 11th A/D Sqdn to check on maintenance. (6) volleyball & other exercise. (7) Shower, shave etc. (8) read a story (9) Supper (10) writing in diary — reading, talking with the different fellows — writing letters — "roger out."

28 November — Flew dawn patrol in which I threw a rod on my left engine. Made it to field okay though. [*In retrospect, I should have feathered my dead engine.*]

Later flew a tracking mission.

29 November — Today I flew a P-40-N on a test hop — I surely had a lot of fun too. Rolls to left and right, then a loop. I had to sweat out the landing. The first time I have flown a conventional l. gear for a long time.

2 December 1944 — Snafu mission to Kendari. Later had a test hop — new camera K-24, so I tried it out. I went to Samate [*airstrip*] and Jeffman [*Island off the northern part of New Guinea*] . . . gave them a time. Also strafed & took pictures of the two airstrips, also a picture of Sarong area & Jeffman really was pouring the lead at me. I returned to the field & took more pictures, hit another tree while strafing today.

3 December — Lt. Garrett of 6th KIA — Kendari. . . .

4 December — . . . Pictures I took the other day didn't pan out, I am afraid. Darn it. . . . [*Wouldn't you know they had put the film in backwards and only one picture out of the bunch was any good. What a disappointment that was after all that risk.*]

5 December — . . . I am definitely going home without my Captaincy, which is the way I wanted it. As I plan now I'll be home in March. . . .

6 December — Today I checked out in a UC-64 [*single-engine aircraft used to carry VIPs around the islands*] — nearly ground looped. . . . Had a scramble today for a Jap photo plane — but couldn't catch him. . . .

7 December — I didn't do anything today. This morning Morriss and Cunningham saw a P-47 flip over on its back at Morotai — pilot was killed of course. He undershot the field & knocked off his l. gear. He had full belly tanks which probably increased his stalling speed. . . .

9 December — Went on Cat cover to Ceram and Boroe. Everything went well enough. We were five minutes early for rendezvous. The mission was about 5 and a half hours. . . .

10 December — . . . Today I flew a test hop and a tracking mission. . . .

11 December — . . . Tonight Lt. Den Raymond is lost — took off from Morotai at 1700. The search lights have been on most of the evening. . . .

I don't see how anyone can get lost between here and there [*from Middleburg Island to the Halmahera Islands*]. . . .

12 December — The search for Raymond today was negative. I took off with Lt. McBride & two others. Three had to return to base — I went on alone. Many planes searched this morning — several this afternoon. An empty life raft was sighted. I am afraid that is the end of Don. It seems that the DF [*Direction Finding*] station gave him a reciprocal course. Until they saw their mistake he had gotten all turned around & was out of range — even his emergency IFF [*Identification Friend or Foe*] couldn't give them a fix on him. He was low on gas — his engine was giving trouble & he said he was going to ditch (water land) it. To ditch a F P-38 at night is out of the question. Why didn't he bail out!! I saw a whale today. Gee he was big.

15 December — . . . Snafu mission (weather) to Palaau again. Returned before getting even as far as Morotai. This afternoon [*a captain*] went on a "Snooper" raid. He was shot up at Sarong: That still remains to my notion the most accurate A/A I have ever seen in my life. No news tonight for us. The big event — 43 enlisted men received word that they are on the list to go home!!

17 December — Spent the entire day flying the L-5 Stinson [*a small plane*] to and from the mainland, carrying passengers and mail etc. Had a lot of fun in it just fooling around. Just heard that Lt. Bradshaw was killed in a L-5 just fooling around with it. A word to the wise is sufficient I hope.

21 December — [*We were each loaded with two 165 gal. of*] Napalm Jel (fire bombs) to hit Japs in Wasili Bay — 12,000 of them stationed rather concentrated there. . . . We loaded up with 1,000# bombs & dive bombed Lolobata. . . . Many, many planes hit the target today. Many large fires were started — Much AA — several boys were holed — one emergency landing at Morotai — Plane & pilot okay.

23 December — Another very good mission or rather two more. Fire bombed Lolobata airdrome areas. Golly we had a lot of fun. The fires were terrific. I got an A/A position. The A/A of course was heavy moderate & fairly accurate. A large shell tore a large hole in Morriss's wing tip. He got home okay though — we went on to Morotai & picked up two more fire bombs. Planes all over the place. Beaufighters, P-40s, P-38s & B-25s. Of course Morotai was the usual mess with about four accidents while I was there. . . . Lt. Rowe is going to Nadzab to instruct "yardbirds.". . .

26 December — Today I am not doing anything, still quite grieved over the loss of Lt. Morriss. Christmas Eve we were standing alert — Dawn patrol got three of us. We went to search Mega village as requested, then searched down the north coast of New Guinea. We spotted two Japanese barges. I climbed up to call to get permission to sink them. After getting permission Lt. Brannon by mistake flew over Doom Island [*off New Guinea*]. He was hit in his right wing — I came home with him & he landed single engine. Lt. Morriss went ahead & strafed one of the barges. Later we were scrambled to go back & get the other barge. By that time it had already gotten to Sarong. We finished off the 1st barge. We then strafed Samate. Morriss wanted to go into Sarong but I thought it was too "hot" in there, so talked him out of that. He and I started home but he said he knew of a gun position that he wanted to strafe & told me to stay away while he went in on it. I would not do that so followed him in. To my surprise, Jeffman [*a bad place to be*]. We turned & I strafed on the way out. A large pier & building there which exploded & burned. He hit something that also burned with large brown smoke. We were very excited. We were orbiting out over the water watching the fire when he started getting in closer to shore. The guns opened up over him. I called and told him that they were firing like hell at him & get away. He replied, "I know it." Immediately after that he was hit in the right boom wheelwell & wing. He caught fire & turned back out to sea. He feathered his r. engine & tried to gain altitude. He couldn't do that. He had already unfastened his harness but still didn't want to get out at so low an altitude. I told him to water land it but he didn't want to with his harness off. I tried to contact him again and again — to do something quick. He acknowledged but did nothing, not knowing what to do. [*By then his engine was on fire. From the time the shell hit his plane, he had about 90 seconds to live. He couldn't bail out because every time he turned loose of the controls the plane would try to auger into the ocean. He was too low to bail out. The longer he waited to water land the less his chances of survival, as the fire was burning explosively. If he got out too quickly he would not be far enough from shore and the enemy would be out there in their motor launches to get him; I could* *only hold them off so long until I ran out of gas. Rescue planes were too far away. We lost radio communication with each other, but I flew right beside him for as long as I could. We both felt so helpless. I am sure we must have prayed. His plane got slower and slower until my plane was trying to stall. I pulled away in the final seconds. The reality of war became very plain to us.*] His boom was burning badly, also his gas tank — then the plane started getting out of control. He leveled it out several times — the last time he leveled it out it stalled and hit the water — exploded & burned. I stayed until the fire died away — nothing remained above the water. I proceeded home, called Fighter control & gave them the information. I was met at the plane by the flight surgeon & intelligence officers & others concerned with the accident. Everyone has been wonderful to me. I was given Amytal & put to bed — where I slept for all that day & part of the next. I did get up & go to church Christmas. I am still very sad and blue about it all. (We had flown together nearly 10 months) Especially so because I was the flight leader. The best of wing men and a wonderful fellow. He was older than I, married & had a little girl. I must close now.

Note: 44th sqdn: lost 4 more planes and pilots in weather returning from the Philippines.

AFTER THIS MISSION I was sent on Rest Leave in Sydney to recuperate. There were no more diary entries until 13 January.

13 January 1945 — . . . Have 4 new boys in the sqdn!! Hooray. I ran into several old cadet classmates while in Sydney. . . . I learned of Marcus Lightfoot's death over Balikpapan. . . .

Major Endress, C.O. 339th Sqdn. shot down at Kendari.

15 January — . . . The rest of our replacements came in yesterday. A very nice boy has moved into our tent. My flight now is composed of myself, Lt. [*Ray*] Nish, Lt. Belue & Lt. Roos. I hope it will be a very good flight — I also hope that I won't be too eager yet at the same time not too cautious.

1st Lieutenant Ray Nish in front of his P-38, "Lil Steve," during his combat tour in the Pacific. The author notes, "Nish was a good man to have in your flight and a good friend."

Jerome A. "Mike" Mykkeltvedt and the author were assigned this plane. They took turns; he flew it one day and Gaskill the next until Mykkeltvedt landed it in the ocean. He was picked up but later killed in another crash.

Captain John Stege, CO of the 68th Fighter Squadron, had much experience in both North Africa and the South Pacific.

17 January — . . . They haven't found Major Endress yet. Stege promoted to Major. Captaincys for Lilly, Leidy, Henkey, & Olson.

18 January — I flew with the new boys. They did okay too except when we got in weather. . . . Major Shapiro returned from Tacloban with all the news — a lot of which I won't write in this diary tonight. . . .

19 January — Went on a strafing mission in Waigeo. New pilots did fine.

20 January — Been overseas one year & 1 month now. Don't know how much longer I'll be over here. Today I screwed up from the word go. First I took off in formation which was a direct disobedience of an order. Second, we were scissoring when my wing man spun out of a tight turn — McBride was leading the flight. I got the blame for it from the C.O. I still don't know why. . . . The last flight went off okay with Capt Hernden leading, except we landed in the rain — the runway was very slick. Lt. Rowe just came in with several other P-40s, one of which nosed over. . . .

21 January — Went on a fire bomb mission to Ceram. Weather caused us to turn back & go to Waigeo. McBride's Napalm Jel bomb exploded when it hit a cocoanut tree — I ran into the flame & explosion. [*I couldn't avoid it.*] The heat was terrific & it burned the paint off the front of my airplane & the rest of it was black. Lt. Nish had started out with us but had to turn back — engine trouble. I couldn't jettison my bomb so had to land with a hung fire bomb — something I surely dreaded — got along okay though. [*When I returned to base, the tower told me to bail out over the ocean. I talked them out of that so they cleared the strip of everything so I could come in with a loaded bomb. It was blackened and so was my plane. I sure dreaded that it might turn loose on the strip and that would be something. But it didn't and I got along okay. You might say I saved a plane and a bomb.*]

22 January — . . . Everything okay in Sqdn except for one enlisted man who was quite haughty. I really "racked him back" yesterday when he made a sneering remark to one of our new pilots about our missions. I put him in his place — our old men & crew chiefs <u>never</u> grumbled about extra work caused by extra training flights. And these new fellows just got off on a bad start.

23 January — Lt. Mahoney, new fellow in 339th, KIA — mushed into building at Ceram [*couldn't pull out in time*]. Lts Nish, Sparks & Minton flew to Ceram today. It was another Cat cover. The mission so far as I was concerned was excellent in that it was the first good mission I have had with my wing man. They did swell — we hit about as bad weather as I have ever been in. We were two minutes late to rendezvous. Dumbo never did get all the way there because of bad weather. We then flew to Kasa isle, a tiny islet inside a large bay. The weather socked in there something fierce & we barely got out of there. Had to go thru a pass in the mountains with the weather down to 1500 ft & less with rain and squalls all around. We made it okay & had to fly on the deck for the next thirty minutes following coastlines etc. We were flying 90 degrees off course to get around the weather. We would go in a place to find it closed in, so we would turn around and try another way out. I repeat, considering everything the mission went off swell — 4 hrs & 5 minutes. They flew close formation and at no time did I have to wonder where they were. Bad cross wind when we landed. I made an excellent landing. Ray didn't do quite so well — he was having trouble with his wheels anyway. I must have been on the ball today for a change. A storm came up tonight. No mail tonight — lovely letters last night.

We [*U.S. Forces*] are now just a few miles from Clark Field!! "Goodow." Lt. Joe Owens returning home (USA) in the morning — hooray!

24 January — . . . no mission at all today. . . . Russians nearing Berlin.

25 January — Flew the piggy back today with Lt. Alter as passenger. He really got a work out. He was a very sick boy when he came down. I guess I was a bit rough on him, but it really makes me mad when someone comes up to me and brags "You can't make me sick." Because anyone will get sick if the pilot wishes it so. That goes for me or anyone else who would be a passenger. [*He had been so rough on the enlisted men that they welcomed this little episode. He was a much easier man to get along with after this. The Assistant Commanding Officer heard about the upcoming flight. He came up to me and whispered, "Are you taking this man up?" I said, "Yes, Sir." He whispered, "Don't come back until he is sick, and that is an order." We flew over to New Guinea, down the canyons, over the mountains, rolls and loops. He pointed to the field; he was very sick.*

So I just did barrel rolls over the airfield and came down to land. He threw up all over me. He missed his bucket. The Flight Surgeon was disgusted at me and took the poor guy to the hospital. I was nearly grounded for that.]

26 January — Started on mission to Philippines. I had to return because of an air lock in the left engine. Confound it!

Ray blew a tire on takeoff, skidded to return, made a beautiful landing on the mat — it was perfect [*I had been called to the tower to assist in any instructions for him*].

Out of eight that took off, four of us returned because of mechanical failure. Poor maintenance.

27 and 28 January — (nothing on the 27th) — Today I flew up to Morotai with Capt. Hernden and got some parts and hydraulic fluid for which we are desperate. I took one P-38H up and brought back a P-38J-15 — a "clinker" too. It was cutting out on the way back. Believe move is off for awhile.

1 February 1945 — Lt. Simpson shot down in Balikpapan by 2 Oscars. Tried to water land the plane but went in with it. Took T/Sgt. MacCormick up in the piggy back. Made takeoff — 80 mph & climbed — 100 mph. It is the most beautiful flying ship, old as it is. I did rolls, loop & Immelman — and buzzing. He was thrilled, no end. Tight turns with delayed use of maneuver flaps — pulls the plane around so tight that it is hard to keep from blacking out. It is about the most maneuverable plane I have flown in a long time.

3 February — Flew 4C-64. Passed 1000 hrs [*flying time*] without an accident [*half of this was combat time*].

5 February — Snafu mission to Balikpapan, returned. Coffelt cracked up on landing; he barely got out with bruises & burns — plane demolished — landing with full ? belly tanks — no brakes, half flaps. I think we all learned or at least had impressed upon us a fact or two. We have been a bit lax lately, I believe. A B-25 crashed in the hills recently, killed several Cols., Lt. Cols., Majors., and Lt. Wells, test pilot, in Fighter Command. I took Capt. Jarrell up piggy back yesterday afternoon.

Met Sgt. Jack Darrow [*a schoolmate of mine from Deming*] today in 18th Airdrome Sqdn. (Capt Walters — C.O.) We have been serviced by that sqdn. for many missions, but today is the first time I saw Jack! He looked fine. [*He may have serviced my plane in times past, I don't know. I later took him up piggy back.*] . . . .

6 and 7 February — Returned today from a long mission. Ray was "snafu" just a hundred miles from target & I returned with him — bad weather. Just my luck! They ran into several Jap planes & got two probables. Naturally!! Confound the luck! . . .

18 February — We have been busy ? moving. Since my last entry Lt. William Benton Hyde (Chicago) was killed over Mindanao. . . . A bomber pilot checked out in a P-38 of 67th Sqdn & he was a real "hot rock" until he augered in!! I think he was a Major. Today the wing commander (Australian) flew my plane — he got along okay they say. Yesterday we flew a review for Maj-Gen [St. Clair] Streett. I led Dancer White flight. The group looked pretty sharp, if I do say so myself. There were numerous accidents at the strip today but so far as I know everyone got out okay. I have practically stopped flying — about two or three hours in the past week.

It rains here every day and as often as a dozen times per day, I do believe. We are living in a transient camp but it isn't bad at all. The chow has really been on the ball. I am feeling in good health and am in good spirits.

See Jack Darrow almost every day now. The Red Cross here is swell and meets us (as we return from missions) with coffee, cold juice, & doughnuts. They are really nice to us too.

A P-40 went in today — I don't know who he was. A very beautiful night — the moon is very bright. Have been to several good shows here.

24 February — Still nothing much has happened here. B-24 exploded on takeoff this morning, and we all jumped out of bed and went over to eat breakfast! I took Capt Underwood, Dallas, Texas, up the other day. Then today I took Jack Darrow up. He really got a kick out of it, I hope. On the 21st I flew with my flight for the first time: Gaskill, Nish, Belue, Roos. We had a very good work out. Weaving & scissoring — it was just a c. training mission. They are real good men.

The mud in this transient camp gets consistently worse. There are nearly 2,500 men in this tiny mud hole and the chow has gotten terrible since the 42nd Bomb Group moved in. They too are on their way to Shangrila!

5 March 1945 — Still here in Morotai. Went to Biak recently for new planes but didn't do any good. I flew a little bit in a B-24 coming home. The operations down in Biak surely screwed up when they let three B-25 boys ferry three new P-38s up the other day. They all went in the drink. One boy was picked up. Hardships! Some hot rock P-51 pilot screwed up and landed on Lolobata, enemy held strip 45 miles from here. [*A lieutenant*] in the 67th sqdn bailed out in traffic pattern. Got in a spin, bad weather. It also was a brand new plane! Oh yes, didn't get the DFC [*Distinguished Flying Cross*] for Tarakan deal, instead got the soldiers medal. Hardship! Guess what, only rained once today and none yesterday! the first dry days we have had.

17 March — Have been doing nothing — still here, awaiting orders. Ferried war weary planes to Biak. The other day Pischke and Schmidt were lost in weather. Three others with them got in okay but Pischke & Schmidt water landed and were picked up. Out of 15 new P-38s coming in the Squadron, only 10 have reached us so far. New pilots dumped them in the drink.

Yesterday was the big mission. We got 5 planes & 1 probable. Nish, Henkey, Shaeffer, Olson, Mykkeltvedt (probable), & Ryzek, all at Balikpapan. [*I did not get to go on this mission.*]

Much grief was suffered by 42nd Bomb Group when they lost their Group C.O., Deputy C.O., and Group Navigator in a plane crash; also several planes have exploded on takeoff lately. The most tragic was a C-47, blew up with the crew & flight fellows on their way home. <u>All were killed</u>.

18 March — This morning Jack Coffelt had another accident when r. motor cut on takeoff & he went into ditch. He was luckier this trip though & didn't get a scratch.

20 March — Woody Woodruff was just killed on takeoff. The engine caught fire.

Had bomb raid — the new fellows were really scared, as if I weren't!!

Arrived in Biak 23 March. Awaiting trip home.

AS I STUDY MY flying log book of over 50 years ago, I see that when I went overseas I had logged 435 hours of training time; of that time, 203 hours were in fighter planes. While there, I flew 604 hours; 522 were combat time.

Overseas, I first logged the total time I flew each day and not the individual flights — test hops, etc. Later, I changed to logging individual flights, *i.e.*, dive bombing, strafing, test hops, patrol, ferrying, etc. I flew 87 missions in P-39s and 90 missions in P-38s.

My log book tells me the number of hours we flew, in what plane, and what we did. We filled out a similar pilot's log in the plane to be picked up each day and taken to the Operations Office for the Air Force records for each pilot. Also after each mission, we filled out a log book for the plane itself, which told the time of departure and return, what was done on the mission, plus remarks about that particular plane — such things as engine sluggish, flaps inoperative, fluid leaks, guns jammed, magnetos dropping rpm, or anything of that nature. This log stayed with each plane for use by the engineering crew to keep track of its flight hours, operation, repairs, and maintenance.

We had excellent maintenance service on our planes in the 68th Fighter Squadron. The crew chiefs and mechanics sweated out every mission we made. They had pride in their work. Sometimes they would work all night to have a plane back in the morning and ready for operation, full of fuel, oil and coolant, ammunition and bomb load, pre-flighted and ready for takeoff.

Sometimes I would have to test fly one before letting it go on a mission. A test flight might take only 25 minutes, or sometimes up to an hour, depending on what the Engineering Officer or I wanted to know.

Our fighter missions in P-39s were only about one or two hours' duration, with a very few exceeding three hours, and that was stretching the limit of its range. One flight to Rabaul was three hours and twenty minutes. We must have carried belly tanks to go that far. On the P-39Q-10 we held only 120 gallons of gas internally.

When we changed over to P-38s, our combat missions were four or five hours or longer. My longest mission was eight hours, plus I landed, refueled, and flew another hour and a half. The mission from Morotai to the Philippines was seven hours and some minutes.

The weather in New Guinea would change rapidly. We lost more planes and pilots to weather and running out of gas over the ocean than we did in combat. Sometimes we turned back, and other times we would find our way through, under, around, or over a weather front. A typical example is my entry for 21 September 1944. It tells of my flight's persistence when others turned back. The CAT we were to provide escort for had also turned back because of weather, so we resorted to strafing secondary targets. The Commanding Officer was pleased, but the Operations Officer was getting worried about us — time, five hours forty minutes; distance 520 miles one way.

Typically, on a return trip, we could relax and appreciate our surroundings. Often we could see a mountain on the horizon, a beautiful sight after going 400 or 500 miles or more to a target. I would check frequently to see if my men were still with me. Sometimes on the way home we would drop down and strafe a secondary target, a Japanese supply base or an airfield.

As we neared mountains, the tropical forest would look so green, velvety, and beautiful. But to the Marines, sailors, soldiers, and anyone else down there, it was mud, filth, dysentery, disease, mosquitoes, malaria, few supplies, short rations, the enemy, and blood and guts. Their weather report might read "clear and still": mud clear up to your butt and still raining! War ain't no fun.

Then as storm clouds would roll in, the mountains would suddenly disappear. What was so beautiful turned ominous. The air would become rough. Everyone would close up because it was safer to fly that way, even in the rough weather. It would get dark, and the lightning would flash all around. We would turn our wing lights on. I would go on instruments, everyone depending on my skill at instrument flying. All eyes would be glued to the nearest man in front. We would be so close to each other that the prop tip wash from my wing man's plane would dip me toward him for a fraction of a second — that's just a little too close. It would make my heart skip a beat!

We would plow on through the storm. I would try to call in, but the radio would be garbled. Where had the mountains gone? We surely didn't want to meet one head on at this stage of our lives. The P-38 was such a stable airplane, but being in a storm wasn't the best place to be, even in that plane.

Some pilots would say our flying was "hours and hours of boredom with a few moments of stark terror!" Everyone would be low on gas; we might have spent too long over the target. But we would stay together. If we could no longer see each other, we would have to separate; then it would be every man for himself on instruments. That could be bad because some of the pilots had not had much instrument flying time and they might just disappear. So hopefully, we would be able to stay together.

All of a sudden there might be a little break in the clouds, and ahead would be our tiny little island and airstrip. I would be grateful that my navigation had been right on! "Collie base, this is Dancer Red One, request straight-in approach." The request would be granted. It would be raining hard, and we would drop down on the deck for better visibility. If the ocean were calmer, we could have seen little whirlwind sprays off of the water from the tips of the plane's propellers ahead of us. Now that was flying low! But at least it would provide a "bottom line" to go by.

We would pull up some and turn a little. We would not do our regular traffic pattern and peel off because some might not have enough gas left to go around. We would let down our wheels and flaps and begin to drop back in trail formation, spacing ourselves for landing. Those lowest on gas would land first; the others would go around. The tower would turn on the few little strip lights for just long enough for us to get down. Home one more time! You would gain respect and admiration for each other on missions like that.

Once we had a very long mission scheduled to go to Borneo. Lieutenant Colonel Shapiro was leading this mission, and it was over 1,900 miles. There were many planes involved. A few hundred miles out, a new pilot began having engine trouble. The group leader called and told me to escort the crippled plane back home. I surely hated to miss out on this mission, as it promised to be one of the best (and was), but we couldn't send a crippled plane back alone. Because I was a test pilot and had flown many trips by myself to get parts, ferry planes, and the like, I was like an old mule — I could always find my way home! Also, if the pilot went down, I could call Air Rescue for help and either circle over him until they came or lead them back to him. So I turned back with him, wondering if he would make it.

As we neared home, I called, "Mayday! Mayday! permission for straight-in approach."

The tower called back and said, "We have planes taking off; circle the field." I thought my buddy probably couldn't make it around the field, that he had been lucky to have gotten that far.

As I contemplated what to do, I heard him say to the tower, "I have turned my gun sights on you, and I am coming straight in."

Boy, that got their attention! The tower looked like a Christmas tree — flares went off, green and red lights flashed, and planes scattered off the strip. He let down his wheels and flaps, came straight on in, and was okay. We were called on the carpet for that, as a formality, but the brass understood the situation and we heard no more about it.

Sometimes we would have a new tower crew that just didn't seem to understand the situation. Don't get me wrong, most of the time they did a wonderful job. I am sure it must have been very stressful for them, what with crippled planes, planes out of gas and other emergency landings, and planes trying to take off, often all at the same time — not to mention occasionally being shot at by the enemy.

All said and done, it took a great deal of cooperation among many people to survive and to accomplish our mission.

Chapter 7

Milestones of the War in the Pacific

AS THE ALLIES sought to counter Japanese aggression in the South Pacific, there were many significant events.

Doolittle's Raid on Tokyo

On 18 April 1942, while the Battle of the Philippines was going on, Major General James H. "Jimmy" Doolittle took off from the carrier USS *Hornet* (referred to as "Shangri-la") with 16 B-25s headed for Tokyo 700 miles west. They were not catapulted, and with all the power they could muster, and being overloaded with fuel, they staggered off the decks on a one-way trip. They took off too soon, because they were spotted by Japanese boats and General Doolittle thought he had lost the element of surprise. But it was a surprise to the Japanese nation!

When these planes arrived, the people initially waved at the low-flying bombers until they realized they were being attacked. In an instant, they realized their country was no longer invincible. Not that much damage was done, but the Japanese suddenly found out they would have to provide more for defense at home, leaving less for aggression on other shores.

This was an enormous morale booster for America. The planes were supposed to land in China, but many ran out of fuel and pilots had to bail out or ditch. Of the 80 airmen in the raid, 71 survived the mission and were picked up by the Chinese. Three were executed by the Japanese. The rest were missing. This event was small in comparison to the bigger battles that were fought later, yet it was a turning point for America.

Battle of the Coral Sea

Soon after Doolittle's Raid, the Battle of the Coral Sea, on 7-8 May 1942, was the first in history where the ships never saw each other, but the planes from the carriers engaged each other. We lost the aircraft carrier *Lexington*, an oiler, and a destroyer. The Japanese also lost several ships, including the carrier *Shoho* and its planes and pilots.

Not knowing that the *Lexington* had gone down and that the aircraft carrier *Yorktown* was damaged, the Japanese returned, thus abandoning the planned invasion and capture of Port Moresby, in New Guinea, and Guadalcanal.

The Japanese didn't know that they could have won that battle and proceeded with their landing. They had won so many battles so easily that they had become over-confident and somewhat careless. Thus Coral Sea really surprised them.

The Australians and New Zealanders still believe the Japanese could have successfully invaded them, and so these countries really appreciate the United States for turning back the enemy at this battle.

Battle of Midway

On 6 June 1942, the Japanese landed on the Aleutian Islands off of Alaska, which scared many in the United States. But, in the end, more troops were lost there on both sides because of the windy, cold weather than were lost in combat.

About 2,000 miles southwest of the Aleutians was Midway Island, about a third of the way from Pearl Harbor to Japan. Just about at this same time, Admiral Chester W. Nimitz was trying to figure out what Admiral Isoroku Yamamoto, the Japanese Naval Commander, was going to do. We had broken the Japanese code and suspected that they were referring to Midway as their main objective. But to check that out, to be absolutely sure, the men at Midway were instructed to flash a radio message that their water treatment plant and machines were broken down.

Immediately the Japanese naval siginals repeated this information, using the code name AF. We had done it! From then on, when the Japanese referred to AF, we knew they were headed to Midway.

What an armada that was! There were at least eight battleships and four cruisers, along with four carriers and other ships. They vastly outnumbered anything we could send against them. One account states that the Japanese had assembled over 86 warships, including transports with thousands of troops, with which they would invade Midway. The attack was to come in two waves: first, the invasion forces accompanied by their carriers with fighter and bomber aircraft, followed by the giant Japanese battleships and cruisers that would wipe out our Navy. However, bad weather had delayed refueling of the second wave of the armada, and they were too far behind to assist their carriers.

Our significantly smaller fleet that was rushing to Midway consisted of only 8 cruisers, 15 destroyers, 3 carriers, and no battleships (they had mostly all been sunk at Pearl Harbor). The aircraft carrier *Yorktown* had been hastily patched up following the Coral Sea battle.

Early in the fight, our forces scored no hits on the enemy. Of our 41 torpedo bombers, 35 were shot down, and the first torpedoes were mostly duds. Many of our planes from Midway were old, obsolete, antique F2A Brewster Buffaloes, which were no match for the Japanese Zeroes. It looked as though the Americans might lose it all.

Within minutes, however, fighter planes and dive bombers from the *Yorktown* and the *Enterprise* spotted the Japanese carriers and dived on them from 14,000 feet. The Japanese carrier *Akagi* (Nagumo's flagship), was hit by a bomb, and fires and explosions followed. Within a few minutes, 54 American pilots destroyed three Japanese carriers. The *Kaga*, *Soru*, and *Akagi* were sunk, and finally so was the *Hiru*. Every carrier in

Nagumo's fleet was destroyed. The Japanese planes then followed our Navy planes back to the *Yorktown* and bombed and torpedoed it until it had to be abandoned. It was finally sunk by a Japanese submarine.

Two Japanese destroyers collided during the melee, and our dive bombers from the USS *Enterprise* finished off the stricken ships. Admiral Nagumo was so shaken by this defeat that he retired his fleet to the northwest, mistakenly believing that we Americans must have had an enormous fleet.

When Admiral Frank J. Fletcher and Admiral Raymond Spruance left the area, it dashed all hopes Yamamoto had of wiping out the rest of our Navy.

Admiral Yamaguchi, captain of the *Hiru*, having lost face, lashed himself to the mast and went down with his ship; he was joined by Captain Kaku. This left Admiral Yamamoto to report the disaster and to apologize to His Majesty Hirohito.

When our Navy left Pearl Harbor headed for Midway our scout planes had spotted the Japanese armada, and Lieutenant Commander John C. Waldron of Torpedo Squadron 8 attacked with 15 planes. None of their torpedoes exploded. All of them were shot down. One pilot, Ensign George H. Gay, the sole survivor, survived to watch the entire show as he floated in his life vest in the ocean where he was later rescued.

Again, as in the Coral Sea, no surface ships engaged each other. Only bombers, fighters, dive bombers, and torpedo planes fought against each other. Planes from Midway Island and our carriers pounded away.

We were terribly outgunned, but the Japanese made some fatal mistakes. As our scout planes spotted and reported the location of this enormous fleet, deck crews on their carriers were loading bombs. When our scout planes were spotted, Admiral Chuichi Nagumo ordered the fighters and bombers to be rearmed with torpedoes. But it was too late! USN dive-bombers caught most of them on deck totally unprepared. Admiral Alan Kirk called it ". . . the first decisive defeat of the Japanese Navy in 450 years."

The aircraft carrier *Yorktown* was crippled and finally sunk; we also lost a destroyer, 150 planes, and 300 men. The Japanese lost 2 cruisers, 3 destroyers, and 4 carriers, along with 275 planes and 3,500 men or more.

This battle, on 4-5 June 1942, six months after Pearl Harbor, turned the tide, and the balance of naval power was being restored to us. B-17 bombers, B-26 bombers, torpedo planes, dive bombers, and fighter aircraft were all involved, even submarines.

The Japanese immediately retreated across the Pacific. The battleships that were hours behind the carriers did not even participate.

Admiral Raymond Spruance knew when he left Pearl Harbor he could not engage the Japanese surface fleet as he had no battleships, and thus he acted accordingly.

Admiral Yamamoto, who had engineered most of the Japanese naval war effort up to this time, had hoped really to confront our forces, but our Admiral Spruance knew better than to engage the battleships. So he took what was left of our fleet and left the scene as the whole Japanese navy headed back toward Japan.

Admiral Spruance had struck at just the right time and at precisely the right place with the right weapons and fantastic luck. It was evident from that moment that carriers were the capital ships of naval warfare.

Battle of Guadalcanal

The Japanese had seized Guadalcanal in the Solomon Islands in 1942, and had begun an airfield there. This alarmed the Allies and, on 7 August 1942, an American force — mostly Marines — assaulted what came to be known as Henderson Field.

The Japanese responded with 900 of their best soldiers, nearly all of which were slaughtered. Their leader committed hari-kari, and thus the Japanese had suffered their first ground defeat.

After that, the Japanese continued to launch large defensive attacks. The Marines suffered incredible hardships including malaria, dysentery, malnutrition, and other illnesses. There was deep mud everywhere, no dry ground. Our forces ran out of supplies. It looked like early April — Bataan — all over again, when General Wainwright had surrendered to the Japanese. Our Navy lost four of five cruisers trying to bring in supplies. It then wired Marine Major General Alexander A. "Archie" Vandegrift that with so many ships lost, it could no longer support Vandegrift's men and that he had permission to surrender. But the Marines hung on.

Finally, with 17,000 troops on this 7- by 4-mile beachhead, Japanese forces were driven out in February 1943. We lost 2,000 men on Guadalcanal; the Japanese lost 9,000. Three of our cruisers were sunk. On board the cruiser *Juneau*, five brothers of the Sullivan family were killed. Navy policy thereafter disallowed two or more family members serving on the same ship.

Because the United States had the advantage of enormous production and replacement of war materiel, the tide began to turn in our favor.

Two years later, several of us went out into the channel at Guadalcanal, which I believe was labeled "Iron Bottom Sound" for all of those ships that were on the bottom. We boarded some of those destroyers that were still protruding out of shallower water — an almost unbelievable sight!

Battle of New Guinea

In September 1942, the Japanese nearly captured Port Moresby, New Guinea, the world's second largest island, and it took them two years to clear it. We finally pushed the Japanese back and took Buna, their last outpost, on the north coast of New Guinea in December 1942. Had the Imperial Japanese forces taken Port Moresby, it would have been a springboard to Australia and New Zealand. General MacArthur had been so frustrated that he had ordered Lieutenant General Robert Eichelberger and his Army troops to "take Buna or don't come back alive."

Naval Battles of the Solomons

From 9 August to 15 November 1942, there were five large naval battles in and near the Solomon Islands. The main battle was at Guadalcanal, but four others played an important role.

At the costly Battle of Savo Island, 8-9 August 1942, a Japanese night attack was repulsed, but we lost three cruisers.

At the Battle of the Eastern Solomons, 15 September 1942, our forces turned back the Japanese, but we lost the aircraft carrier USS *Wasp* and five destroyers.

At the Battle of Cape Esperance, 12 October 1942, we again drove off the Japanese. They were desperately determined to hold on there and resupply Guadalcanal.

And at the Battle of Santa Cruz Island, 26 October 1942, three enemy carriers and two destroyers were damaged, and we shot down about 100 planes; but we lost the aircraft carrier *Hornet* and destroyer *Porter*, the aircraft carrier *Enterprise* was damaged, and 74 planes were lost.

Battle of the Bismarck Sea

In March 1943, the frustrated Japanese loaded an infantry division of

7,000 troops and equipment in Rabaul, New Britain, en route to Huon Gulf, New Guinea. Eight transports were escorted by four destroyers. As they entered the Bismarck Sea, the U.S. Army 5th Air Force and the Royal Australian Air Force from Papau, New Guinea, sank or severely damaged all of the ships, drowning nearly all of the reinforcements. One report listed 15,000 killed — a smashing victory for the Allies.

General MacArthur's strategy was to capture beachheads and airstrips, set up a perimeter and hold on to it, and bypass the rest of an island. He did not believe we could root out all of the Japanese back in those jungles.

Rabaul became isolated; we just went around it. We pounded away with bombs but didn't land troops there. Likewise, the island of Truk was a very heavily fortified supply base, which we pounded completely out of action and went around.

We went on up the Solomons to Bougainville. Just prior to our taking it, only 16 of our planes had a terrific impact on Japan by the shooting down of Admiral Yamamoto.

The Downing of Admiral Yamamoto

Once again we had broken the code of the Japanese. Admiral Isoroku Yamamoto was going from Rabaul, New Britain, to Kalili Air Field, Bougainville, in the Solomons in April 1943. A coded message was sent giving the exact time of his arrival on Ballale Island nearby. It also said he would be riding in a Betty Bomber and would be accompanied by six fighters (Zeroes).

Admiral Nimitz at Pearl Harbor and Admiral William F. Halsey in the Southwest Pacific had to wire Washington for President Roosevelt's permission to ambush and shoot down Yamamoto.

The Navy had planned to get the Admiral as he was boarding a ship, but Major John W. Mitchell said that the best way was to get him in the air. The Navy did not have planes with long enough range for that mission at that time. USAAF Commander Mitchell and his 339th Fighter Squadron of the 347th Fighter Group, 13th Air Force, was called in from Guadalcanal. I would join the 347th nine months later. Our P-38 compasses were not adequate, so the Navy installed an additional one in Major Mitchell's plane. He worked diligently into the night to route a dog-legged course and schedule. The dog-leg would confuse enemy tracking; the timing had to be perfect.

The distance from Guadalcanal to Bougainville was 436 miles. From Rabaul to Bougainville was 415 miles. Major Mitchell calculated that the Admiral would travel at 180 miles per hour. Mitchell's group would travel at 200 miles per hour in five separate headings. Yamamoto was punctual, and they knew exactly to the minute when he would be arriving at Kalili Airdrome. They had to attack before he landed. There were 75 Japanese Zeroes on the ground that would pounce on our planes if Mitchell was late.

On 18 April, Major Mitchell, with 15 other planes, got off the ground and flew his course. They flew 50 feet off the ocean — at wave-top level — to avoid radar detection. It was hazy. Mitchell approached the coast one minute ahead of the estimated time — miraculous! Admiral Yamamoto was also one minute ahead of time. The timing was exact! "Bogies high at 11 o'clock." Two bombers covered by six Zeroes were preparing to land. The leading bomber (we later found out) carried Yamamoto.

As the P-38s gained altitude, the Zeroes got behind them. Captain Thomas G. Lamphier broke to the left to meet them head on and shot one down. Lieutenant Rex T. Barber slipped in behind the lead bomber and shot it down with Admiral Yamamoto on board (one bullet went through the Admiral's head). The bomber crashed in the jungle. Barber then moved over and helped explode the other bomber. Pearl Harbor was partially avenged.

In the heat of battle, it was and still is unclear who did what. We were thought to have lost one plane and one pilot — Lieutenant Raymond Hine. But that victory must have shortened the war somewhat, and it was a terrible shock to Japan.

Little was known about this mission in the United States, because we didn't want the Japanese to suspect we had broken their code. Years later, one of the accompanying Zero pilots gave his version of this battle, which clarified some of the questions. I believe Major Mitchell's account is probably correct. Two enemy bombers and three Zeroes were shot down.

Admiral Yamamoto had been the one who had engineered the attacks on Pearl Harbor, Midway Island, and other devastating battles against our country. He was a Japanese hero, the commander-in-chief of the Japanese Combined Fleet. Admiral Matome Ugaki, Chief of Staff of the Japanese Imperial Fleet, was in the other bomber that was shot down, at sea, but he and others managed to survive.

Meanwhile, in the Pacific, north of the Equator, Admiral Nimitz was ordered to take back the islands Japan had conquered. South of the Equator, General Douglas MacArthur, backed by Admiral William F. "Bull" Halsey with American and New Zealand troops, was to move up the island chain from the Solomons and New Guinea all the way to the Philippines.

Rabaul, New Britain, was a large stronghold from which the enemy dispatched supplies, troops, and naval power. Far to the northeast, the Japanese captured and held the Aleutian Islands for nearly a year, but finally withdrew on 23 May 1943. Brutal weather there cost both sides dearly.

In June 1943, our forces ran the Japanese out of Rendova Island in the Solomons, then Salamaua, New Guinea. On 17 August, 49 B-24 bombers and 83 P-38 fighters raided Wewak and Boram, New Guinea. The B-25s destroyed 150 of the 225 planes on the ground. The next day saw another raid; P-38s shot down 14 and the bombers got 18 more Japanese fighter planes. The P-38s and the B-25s were getting with it. We were getting more new airplanes all the time. On October 12, 87 heavy bombers, 114 B-25s (medium bombers), and 12 Beaufighters, along with 125 P-38s for cover, shot down 26 Japanese planes and destroyed another 100 on the ground. We lost 2 B-24s, 1 B-25, and 1 Beaufighter to antiaircraft fire. On 25 October, 54 P-38s covered 62 bombers to Rabaul. We shot down 35 planes, and the bombers got 8 more.

The air battle raged on, but Japan kept sending more and more reinforcements to Rabaul. On 2 November, 57 P-38s escorted 75 B-25s to Rabaul. This time the Japanese sent up over 125 fighters. The P-38s shot down 41, and the B-25s got 27 more; we lost 9 B-25s and 9 P-38s, but thousands of tons of Japanese shipping was sent to the bottom that day. The last big raid over Rabaul took place on the 7th of November, costing us 5 P-38s. The seven main strikes had cost us 16 P-38s to 234 Japanese planes. This was all the more remarkable because we had to go such a long distance to attack them.

Along about then, our supply of P-38s dwindled to nearly nothing, and the 39th Squadron and the 9th Squadron had to give their planes to the 475th Fighter Group to replenish their losses. Several squadrons then received P-47 Thunderbolts. These were excellent planes but had a shorter range than our P-38s. Then in December 1943, Allied Forces landed on New Britain Island. Rabaul was so heavily defended that we did not try to capture it, but continued to bomb and strafe it for months.

The Coast Watchers reported that a very large building marked with a white cross showing it to be a hospital was not a hospital. They said that it housed supplies and ammunition, so we blasted it and hoped the Coast Watchers were right. They almost always were. There was more aircraft and antiaircraft artillery fire there than any other place I flew into. I can't figure out how our losses were so light.

The Gilbert Islands in the central Pacific had many of the coral reefs so predominant throughout the South Pacific. The islands were honeycombed with caves and bunkers. Consequently, the Marines met with savage, fanatical suicide attacks. We lost 900 Marines and 2,000 injured there on the Tarawa Atoll and Betio Island, at the southwest tip of Tarawa. This tiny strip of coral became a virtual graveyard. Right off the coast, off Makin Atoll, the escort carrier USS *Liscome Bay* was sunk by a Japanese submarine; 644 men aboard went down with her.

Admiral Nimitz's Navy then went on to the Marshall Islands and took Kwajalein Island in late January 1944. This was the first prewar Japanese-held territory that had been retaken. Our bombardment was so intense that there wasn't much resistance on the landing. As it was the site of a most important airfield for both fighters and bombers, our Seabees went right to work repairing the field, and our planes were landing on it even before the fighting was over.

Our forces then went on to Eniwetok Island, and by 21 February its capture was complete. Parry Island wasn't so easy either, but it was declared secure on 22 February. Also in February, Admiral Spruance headed for Truk in the Caroline Islands. This secretive island was another supply base for all Japanese activity in the South Pacific. There were 30,000 Japanese soldiers garrisoned there. Our planes and ships bombed and shelled it to rubble but did not invade it.

On 15 June 1944, our Marines invaded the island of Saipan in the Mariana Islands. Here, again, the enemy fought viciously from caves and pillboxes. In July, Army Infantry and Marines began the assault on Guam and Tinian Islands; by August, the "mopping up" operations were complete. And by the end of November 1944, our B-29 Superfortresses were flying from Guam and Saipan to bomb Japan.

Battle of the Philippine Sea

On 19 and 20 June 1944, after the Americans took Guam and Saipan, the Japanese decided to counterattack. Vice Admiral Marc A. Mitscher's U.S. Task Force 58 engaged Japan's Admiral Jisaburo Ozawa. The battle is referred to as the "Marianas turkey shoot" because our aircraft shot down 300 enemy planes to our loss of 28. The big carrier *Shokaku*, Ozawa's flagship, was sunk by our submarines. Admiral Ozawa departed from the battle with only 35 of his carrier planes left, and he lost two more carriers — 14 ships. As this battle carried into the night, 73 of our carrier-based planes couldn't find their own carriers and crashed into the sea. The next day, 65 of their aircrew pilots were rescued.

In September 1944, the Marines established a beachhead on Peleliu in the Palau Islands, west of the Philippines, and on the 15th we recaptured Morotai.

In China, the Japanese overran seven Chinese-American bases, but the Chinese finally took them back before the war was over.

Battle of Leyte Gulf

The Japanese knew that MacArthur was determined to return to the Philippines; and they planned a desperate gamble called "Sho-1" (Big Victory).

On 20 October 1944, 700 of our ships arrived in Leyte Gulf. The Japanese challenged our landings there with three battles — at Surigao, Samar, and Cape Engano — collectively known as Leyte Gulf.

The plan was for Admiral Ozawa to take his carrier fleet, which by that time had lost nearly all of its carrier-based planes, and lure Admiral Halsey's Third Fleet to the north away from the support of our landing troops. Halsey took the bait and left his post, so to speak, to go after Ozawa's fleet. Halsey had 6 fast battleships, 8 large attack carriers, 8 light carriers, 15 cruisers, and 58 destroyers.

This left Vice Admiral Thomas C. Kincaid with 6 old, slow battleships, 16 escort carriers (small, slow, converted merchant ships), 11 cruisers and some other ships, PT boats, and submarines to defend our amphibious forces going ashore. Kincaid's battleships got their revenge for Pearl Harbor when the southern Japanese force tried to attack through Surigao Strait and was beaten back by Admiral Jesse Oldendorff's old battleships crossing his T.

Japanese Vice Admiral Takeo Kurita, commanding the Samar or Central Force, headed for Admiral Kincaid with his powerful fleet. Our submarines, *Darter* and *Dace*, put five torpedoes into Kurita's flagship *Atago*, then sank the cruisers *Takao* and *Amaya*. Kurita shifted his flag to a destroyer, then to the big battleship *Yamato*. Kurita charged on toward Kincaid, who was running low on ammunition and supplies. To the north, the fleet engaged the enemy, and U.S. Naval Commander Dave MacCampbell's Squadron knocked down 25 planes with no losses of his own.

The light carrier *Princeton* claimed another 34 planes. Later, it would catch a bomb and sink.

Admiral Kurita's Central Fleet included not only the *Yamato* but also the *Musashi*,the world's largest battleships — the "super battleships." He lost one battleship, four cruisers, and four destroyers, and feared the Third Fleet was going to get him, so he left the battle.

Vice Admiral Shoji Nishimura's flagship (a battleship) was hit, and he also left the battle. Admiral Shima entered the battle scene and, seeing all the destruction, decided that dying for the Emperor was not that great; so he left.

Here, again, the Japanese had all but won the battle, but withdrew. Admiral Ozawa's decoy plan had worked; he had drawn Halsey's Third Fleet away. This fleet could have annihilated the entire Japanese fleet had Halsey not sought to destroy the enemy carriers, always his prime objective. However, the Japanese were not to fight a large engagement again — this was the largest naval battle ever fought.

On 20 October 1944, when General MacArthur's forces landed on Leyte Island in the middle of the Philippines, following heavy air and naval bombardment, the Japanese ground forces were split in half. MacArthur flamboyantly waded ashore and fulfilled his promise of "I shall return." He had the pleasure of liberating some of the beleaguered U.S. prisoners of war.

Tacloban, Leyte, became the temporary capital of the Philippines, and MacArthur helped set up President Osmena and his government.

On 9 January 1945, our forces landed in Lingayen Gulf. From there they moved south to capture Manila, then farther south to retake Bataan and Corregidor, where our ground forces had suffered their first disastrous and bloody defeats three years earlier. The fight for Manila almost destroyed the city. Some 20,000 Japanese soldiers fought on until nearly all were killed. Later, farther south, 50,000 Japanese surrendered.

Kamikaze planes appeared in large numbers in the Lingayen Gulf. They sank 17 U.S. ships and damaged 50 more. On 17 May 1945, the aircraft carrier USS *Franklin* lost 772 men, the result of a Japanese dive bomber.

It took almost a year of hard fighting to liberate the Philippines. In fact, fighting was still going on there when Japan surrendered.

General MacArthur had had a very hard time convincing the War Department to go into the Philippines before invading the islands of Japan. As it turned out, the dropping of the atomic bomb made it unnecessary to continue the war. The battle at Leyte saw us lose 8,500 servicemen as against nearly 55,000 Japanese killed.

It is interesting to note that the Japanese had overwhelmed the Philippines in 1942 by taking control of sea and air power. When MacArthur returned, he had that control. However, against Bataan and Corregidor, he had used naval power and amphibious assaults, which allowed him to strike at his own convenience.

Iwo Jima

Our forces landed on Iwo Jima, directly on course between Guam and Japan, on 19 February 1945. The Japanese fighter planes there could really harass our bombers on the way to and from Japanese targets. It was also important for us to have an emergency landing base for our crippled bombers and a staging area for our fighter planes to cover the long-range B-29s on their bombing missions to Japan. This island was only about 5 miles by 2 miles, but the Japanese had elaborate caves and bunkers as well as the latest in sophisticated weapons.

By the end of the third day of fighting, 1,800 Japanese had been killed; only one had surrendered. In the end, we lost 6,800, mostly Marines, plus about 900 sailors, and 20,000 were wounded. About 22,000 Japanese were killed there, and we captured about 1,000. Probably the most famous picture from the war is the raising of our flag above Mount Suribachi on Iwo Jima.

Okinawa

On 1 April 1945, we landed 50,000 Army and Marine troops on Okinawa, which is about 300 miles south of Japan's Kyushu Island. Bitter fighting went on for almost three months. Almost every American that the Japanese captured was killed. We lost 35 warships, mostly due to kamikaze (suicide fighter bombers) and ohka (one-way mission manned bomb) attacks; 200 others were damaged. At one point, the ratio of Japanese to

American planes lost was 40 to 1, revealing the desperation of the enemy in launching suicide missions. The aircraft carrier USS *Bunker Hill* was sunk off Okinawa.

Over 107,000 Japanese were killed. Hundreds committed suicide by jumping from cliffs into the sea; estimates were that another 20,000 may have been incinerated in caves.

Our losses were 12,000 soldiers and sailors killed and 36,000 wounded. U.S. Army General Simon B. Buckner, one of the few Generals lost during the war, was killed there.

Nearly one quarter of a million people were killed in and around Okinawa; 150,000 of them were Okinawan civilians. The Japanese lost 5,900 airplanes to nearly 1,000 of our own. By this time, Japan's best pilots were dead.

Target: Saigon

The Saigon mission was flown by Lieutenant Ray Nish after I had left the Squadron to go home. His account, which follows, was published in the 1992 edition of *Lightning Strikes*, an excellent publication of the P-38 National Association. It is reprinted with their permission.

Ray Nish was a fine wing man, a great flier, a credit to our country, who was and still is my friend. I have never known him to exaggerate, so I believe the following to be a true and accurate account. I wish I could have been with them on that mission.

TARGET: SAIGON

by Ray Nish, 68th Fighter Squadron,
347th Fighter Group, 13th Air Force

Our target on April 14, 1945, was Saigon, the Japanese-held capital of French Indochina. It was time, 13th Fighter Command felt for the 13th Air Force fighters based in the Philippine Islands to make an opportunity sweep of the China mainland. They assigned the pioneering mission to the P-38s of the 347th Fighter Group at Puerto Princesa, Palawan.

The 347th's pilots had flown P-39 and P-38 missions from New Caledonia, Guadalcanal in the Solomons, New Hebrides and from New Guinea, the Halmaheras and the Philippines, all over the Coral, Bismarck, Celebes, Sulu, Molucca and Ceram seas, the Makassar Strait, the South China Sea to Borneo targets — 99 percent of them over water. Someone in fighter command, however, decided the flight to Saigon should have a lead navigation plane. Previous flights to Balikpapan, Borneo, took us on longer courses than this one, but still a B-25 from the 42nd Bomb Group was assigned to lead us to this new target. Officially, the mission was fighter escort for the lone B-25.

The flight would take us 850 miles west over the South China Sea and 850 miles back on the return. The flight of eight and one-half hours would be far from the longest we had flown, but the route to the target and return was entirely over water.

The 347th put up two flights of four P-38s each for this mission — five Lightnings from the 68th Fighter Squadron and three from the 339th Fighter Squadron. Two 165-gallon drop tanks provided the range needed. Captain Clyde D. McBride of the 68th was Red leader. I flew as his wingman on this mission. 1/Lt. William G. Keyworth, Jr., also of the 68th, led the 339th pilots.

We got airborne and climbed out to join the B-25. After nearly an hour, two of the 339th planes had aborted, one at a time, for one reason or another. That left six P-38s following a B-25. In addition to McBride, Keyworth and me, the other pilots were David W. Pruess and Robert E. Worthen (68th) and Wayne R. Meyers (339th).

I was tracking the flight path against the course on my map and the B-25 was taking us on a more northerly heading than we had figured. I moved in behind McBride's left wing and caught his glance. Holding up my map, I pointed to the B-25 and shook my head.

Texan McBride broke radio silence: "Ahh know, Ahh'm gonna' give him five more minutes."

The B-25 pilot also broke radio silence; "Is there a problem?"

McBride: "Yeah, you're off course."

B-25 pilot: "Minute, please."

Shortly, the B-25 pilot radioed: "Our nav says we're okay."

Goodbye B-25, Hello Saigon

McBride looked at me. I shook my head. He nodded and six P-38s banked left and held the turn for 30 to 35 degrees before rolling out on a new heading for Saigon.

As expected, our course brought us to the southern tip of Cape St. Jacques and the Japanese airfield just to the north on the peninsula. That airfield was our primary target. We were at 10,000 feet over the mouth of the Mekong Delta under a gray overcast sky and felt cheated. Our searching eyes could not spot a single Japanese plane in the air, on the ground, in the hangars or on the ramp. We later theorized the Japanese had flown their planes to another field because of a limited fuel supply.

After releasing our drop tanks, we followed Red leader into a spiraling dive for the deck and headed for the confluence of two major rivers. McBride led us into a Japanese destroyer docked in the Dong Nai River, with steam up and firing at us. While dodging the destroyer's flak pattern, all of us managed a good strafing run at the port beam.

Pulling up and over the destroyer, we could see several ships at the docks lining the Saigon River near its juncture with the Dong Nai. They were broadside to us. There were cargo ships, some 10,000 tons, some smaller. Down to the water and up the Saigon River we went, spread and in trail. We kept below the treetops that lined the river, pulling up to clear the ships' masts.

We were getting heavy artillery and intense ground fire from both banks of the river, batteries protecting the docks and the several large fuel storage tanks flanking the river. When we ran out of docked ships, we sprayed the fuel tanks and gun batteries. On up the river we flew north of Saigon.

Ahead we saw an explosion as McBride destroyed a Japanese amphibian plane on the river ramp next to the airfield. He led us across the field into a shallow climb for wing-over 180 and, coming back down, all of us got good shots at planes in front of the hangar, as well as the hangar.

McBride nearly flew through the hangar while firing a blast that started it on fire. He turned left into the river for a strafing run back down the river, all of us in trail.

Now the batteries were ready for us and we drew both

artillery and small arms fire again as we made a run at the fuel tanks and gun positions we had seen on the way up the river. Soon we were back to the cargo ships. Two of them were listing, so we pumped some more shells into them.

Ahead was a large fuel tank and I aimed a good blast into it, puncturing it and drawing black smoke. But I noticed that the last 20-mm shells to leave my cannon were spiraling and losing velocity. My next firing told me why: I had burned the riflings and, worse than that, I was now out of all ammo.

"I've been hit!"

Myers, the 339th pilot, pulled up and radioed, "I've been hit!" I could see his left rudder had been cut in half by flak and told him to get down on the river.

We were now down river and approaching that destroyer from its starboard beam. And my ammo was gone. McBride and other pilots strafed it again.

Back to the delta now and still on the deck, we started closing on Red Leader when he called for a run at the flak towers that lined the peninsular tip of land at the mouth of the Mekong. I couldn't do any damage but felt my safety was to stay on the water.

There were four or five gun towers in an arc-like line at Cap St. Jacques, south of the vacated airfield, and our P-38s really blasted them. All but me. As he pulled off the last tower and turned down the delta, McBride said, "Let's do it again!" Keyworth, thinking of Meyers' damage, suggested that we head out and join up.

"Look who's here!"

Red leader soon called out, "Look who's here at 10 o'clock!" Approaching us at about 5,000 feet on a southerly heading paralleling the coast was the B-25 navigation plane.

McBride couldn't resist, "You missed the show, Baker Fox!" No response. That was our last contact with the B-25.

Our P-38s had sunk a medium freighter, destroyed a small freighter, damaged four other freighters, destroyed a seaplane base hangar and one plane, damaged a second hangar, two gun positions and two fuel storage tanks. We couldn't confirm damage to the destroyer.

We climbed to 8,000 feet and held our plotted course for home, nearly four hours away. An hour or so later, Meyers told Red leader his fuel was running low. With the drag from his shattered left rudder, it was no surprise. McBride asked him to read out his fuel gauges. I watched mine as Meyers read his. He had more than I did!. I attempted to ease his anxiety: "You've got more than I have and I plan on making it!"

Even with all the excitement of the Saigon strafing runs, time was now dragging. Nothing but water of the South China Sea below and ahead, and a sky that was hazy.

A half hour out of Palawan, McBride radioed Waitress, our control tower, and reported one damaged Uncle and one low on fuel. The landings were uneventful, although not totally routine for Meyers.

My plane's crew chief later reported I had about 10 minutes more flying time. Close, but with no storms to fly over or around on our return, it was no sweat.

That was the last time fighter command assigned a navigation plane to us.

ON 23 MARCH 1945, I arrived in Biak, awaiting my trip home. We waited quite a while for a ship, a Dutch one carrying former prisoners of war who had been held by the Japanese in the Santa Tomas Prison in the Philippines. It was on the ship that I learned of President Roosevelt's death, in April. He had been a wonderful president.

The food on that ship was out of this world. On the other side of the hold from where I was bunked was a jail-like section that held mental patients. They were screaming and carrying on; what a pitiful sight. I began to question my own sanity. I found out later that I was ultimately sent home because I was suffering from combat fatigue. That was probably true. Toward the end, my attitude probably got worse and worse.

At about this time, the men who wanted to stay in the service received their captain's bars and flew to San Francisco. We all landed there at about the same time — how ironic! What kind of luck was that?

By virtue of the fact that my name started with a "G," I was put in charge of a troop train bound for El Paso, Texas. That was some experience. Can you imagine all of the celebrating that had started after we sailed under the Golden Gate Bridge? I had a difficult time keeping those boys on the train to get them to El Paso.

I arrived at Fort Bliss about 2 a.m. and met my wife at the St. Regis Hotel. It had been 16 months of separation. How wonderful it was!

After a three-week leave at home in Deming, New Mexico, the Army Air Forces gave us an all-expense paid vacation in the Santa Monica Beach Hotel in Santa Monica, California. They asked me if I wanted out of the service, as I had more than the required number of points. Elvena and I talked it over and decided I would get out and we would buy a farm in New Mexico.

I was sent to Camp Beale in Marysville, California, where I was mustered out. So ended my service career.

Chapter 8

Unsung Heroes

AIRPLANES SOMETIMES put up a spectacular show, but the submarines, known as the silent service, really made their mark. In the early days, submarines were thought to provide a poor country protection of its harbors and shores; but during World War II, they became a very important part of the war effort, not only sinking or spying on enemy ships, but also delivering supplies to remote areas and picking up shipwreck survivors or downed pilots.

At the time, nobody knew much about the submarine fleet, because it operated in secret; and the media and our leaders respected that need. The enemy, however, desperately wanted every scrap of information it could get about our undersea fleet.

Submarines sank over five million tons of cargo — 1,314 Japanese vessels, mostly merchant ships accounting for over half of all Japanese shipping, as well as 130 Japanese submarines.

The high, fast-flying special P-38s — F5s, or Photo-Joes, as they were called — did a tremendous job of taking pictures of everything that moved or needed to be moved. We had far better radar, radio communication, and intelligence service than the Japanese, thereby giving us a tremendous advantage. Too bad we didn't have that when Pearl Harbor was bombed, or it would never have happened.

As the war progressed, our planes knocked so many Japanese out of the air that their new pilots were not skilled enough. Their losses began to increase sharply. On a single day, 11 June 1944, American carrier-based planes shot down 97 enemy aircraft; a few days later, we shot down 53 more.

In the South Pacific, the main fighter planes were P-38s, F4Fs, P-40s, P-47s, F6Fs, and P-39s; B-24 bombers also shot down many Japanese fighter planes. P-38s shot down the most Zeroes; P-39s were the worst fighter plane against Zeroes. But the P-39 was an excellent ground support plane, strictly low altitude with no supercharger. In fact, the early models didn't even have oxygen for the pilots. Now how could a fighter pilot get up to an enemy that was flying at 15,000, 20,000, or 25,000 feet?

In aviation terms, an ace is a pilot who has shot down five or more planes confirmed — the pilot or his buddy had actually to see the enemy crash into the sea or ground. This was not always possible because of cloud cover or the confusion of battle. The first priority was to protect your flight leader, yourself, and your buddies. The next was to knock the enemy down. Last was to look to see if your target had "gone in." Later we had nose cameras in the planes, which provided great assistance in identifying the action. As I read the accounts of the different aces, I am struck by the incredible audacity and luck some of them had. They prided themselves on how few rounds of ammunition it took to shoot down an enemy plane and chalk up a "victory." In contrast, when our outfit was strafing a ship or ground target, we poured all the ammunition we could get into it.

Here is a partial list of the "score" of Americans *vs.* Japanese:

Plane	Pilot	Japanese Planes Downed
P-38	Dick Bong	40
P-38	Thomas B. "Tommy" McGuire	38
P-40 & F4F	Gregory "Pappy" Boyington	28
P-38	Charles H. MacDonald	27
F4F	Joe Foss	26
F4F	Robert Hanven	25
P-47	Neal Kearby	23
P-40	Robert L. Scott	22
P-38	Robert B. Westbrook, Jr.	20
F4F	Ken Walsh	20
P-38	Tommy Lynch	20
F4F	John Smith	19
F4F	Marion Carl	18
F4U	Ike Kepford	17
P-40	Tex Hill	17
F4F	Jim Swett	15
P-38	Porky Cragg	15
P-40 & P-38	Dick West	14
F4F & F6F	Scott McCusky	13.5
P-40	Bob Neal	13
F6F	Wendell VanTwelves	13
F4F	Butch O'Hare	12
F4U	Tom Blackburn	11
P-38	Corky Smith	11
P-38	Bob Aschenbrener	10
P-38	Perry J. Dahl	9
F6F	Dave MacCampbell	9 (1 mission)
F6F	Fred Bakutis	7.5
F6F	Spider Webb	7
P-38	Charles King	7
P-38	John Dear	7
P-38	Jack Purdy	7
F4U	Dewey Dunford	6
F6F	Ralph Hanks	6
P-38	Don McGee	6

Plane	Pilot	Japanese Planes Downed
F6F	Dick May	6
P-38	Jack Jones	5
F4U	Bill Farrell	5
F4U	Joe Lynch	5
F4U	Joe Robbins	5
P-38	Frank Holmes	5
P-40	Jim Morehead	5
F4F	Don Gordon	5
P-51	Randy Reeves	5
F6F	Harry Swinburn	5
F4U & F6F	Bruce Porter	5

and the list goes on . . .

Major Dick Bong became the leading ace in the Pacific with a score of 40 planes to his credit; he crashed in 1945, and was killed in 1945 testing a P-80 jet in the United States.

Major Thomas B. "Tommy" McGuire had 38 to his credit before he crashed in the jungle while going to the aid of another pilot.

Charles MacDonald, while commanding the 475th Fighter Group, shot down 27 planes.

Lieutenant Colonel Robert B. Westbrook, Jr., shot down 20 Japanese planes in the South Pacific before he was killed by a heavily armed Japanese gunboat in the Makassar Strait east of Borneo. He was our 13th Air Force hero; besides his aerial accomplishments, he inflicted untold damage to Japanese ground and sea targets while dive bombing and strafing in his P-38. The missions I flew with him leading were always interesting, to say the least, and we were very sad when he went down.

Scott McCusky shot down at least 13 planes, but only one 7.7mm Japanese bullet ever hit his plane. This was at the Battle of Midway when he was flying off of a carrier in an F4F.

Lieutenant Jack Jones shot down his first Zero while flying a P-39 (P-400). It turned out that the Japanese pilot Jones shot down was a 15-kill ace for the Japanese Imperial Navy. The doomed Japanese pilot crawled out onto the wing of the burning, diving plane as it crashed. He had no parachute, because it was considered to be beneath the dignity of the samurai warrior to wear one. Jones's other kills were made while flying P-38s.

John Galvin was shot down but picked up under adverse conditions at sea by our submarine *Harder*. He was returned sometime later to his squadron; however, shortly after that, the *Harder*, with its Commander Sam Dealy, was sunk by Japanese depth charges. The *Harder* had sunk seven Japanese destroyers in its short life of a few months.

Ralph Hanks, flying off the carrier USS *Lexington II* near Tarawa, shot down five Japanese planes on one mission, becoming an ace in a single day.

Dick West, of the 35th Fighter Squadron, 5th Air Force, shot down 14 confirmed victories and 3 probables. He also helped burn a Japanese tanker and wipe out a bridge. He was shot down in Mindanao, Philippines, but was rescued by friendly guerrillas and returned to his outfit.

Jack Purdy, of the 475th AAF Group, destroyed seven planes but crash-landed four times. He flew 184 combat missions in a P-38.

Captain Bob Aschenbrener, of the 49th Fighter Group, was shot down in the Philippines, injuring his back, after flying 345 combat missions and shooting down 10 planes. Guerrillas carried him out part way on a carabao (water buffalo).

Commander Fred Bakutis had 7.5 kills and was shot down while he was strafing a destroyer, but he managed to get out and into a life raft. He was adrift for six days before being picked up by our sub, the *Hardhead*.

U.S. Navy **Lieutenant John Dear** had a score of seven in the daytime, but his main missions were night patrols in F6Fs.

I cannot figure out how the Japanese with all their powerful fleet and their fast, maneuverable Zero fighter planes lost so heavily to us. Certainly, it was a credit to our forces. In the beginning, their Zeroes could outmaneuver and fly higher and faster than anything we had. We were also outnumbered. But little F4Fs and P-40s could take a lot more punishment because our pilots were protected by an armor plate behind the pilot's head, back, and bottom; and the fuel tanks were rubberized and self-sealing so they didn't blow up like those in the Japanese planes. Also, our 50-caliber and 20mm cannon were far superior to theirs. Many of the Japanese planes blew up when hit by our guns. With no armorplate protection behind the pilots, many of them were killed by our pilots who aimed right at that Achilles heel. The Japanese had gained their great maneuverability by sacrificing safety to save weight. After we got bigger and better planes, the odds changed rapidly, but the enemy's planes were being improved, too.

Major General James H. "Jimmy" Doolittle was not an ace, but he was awarded the Medal of Honor for his daring raid on Japan, which was our first spark of hope after the Pearl Harbor disaster. Although Doolittle himself considered the mission a failure, it was a great boost for America. He was later to command 2,000 bombers and 1,400 fighter planes in the 8th Air Force.

In the Pacific Theater there were 221 Medal of Honor recipients. Over half of these were awarded posthumously. All of these people went "above and beyond the call of duty."

One of the first to come to mind is **General Jonathan M. Wainwright** who, with his 71,000 American and Filipino troops and obsolete equipment, held off 250,000 well-armed Japanese troops until he ran out of food, supplies, and medicine. Had it not been for Wainwright and his troops keeping the Japanese occupied there, I believe the enemy would have gone on to take Australia, New Zealand, and perhaps the rest of the Pacific — and who knows what next. General Wainwright thought he had failed. But he and his men were all heroes. After three years of torture and starvation, he was released from a Japanese prison camp at the end of the war, and President Harry Truman presented him with the Medal of Honor.

Another, **Colonel Gregory "Pappy" Boyington**, formed Marine Squadron 214 (the Black Sheep Squadron). Those 49 pilots shot down 97 planes confirmed and 35 probably destroyed. Boyington shot down six planes while he was with the Flying Tigers, then 22 more in the Pacific. He was shot down and presumed dead and was awarded the Navy Cross and the Medal of Honor "posthumously." But he had been picked up by a Japanese submarine, survived their brutality, and was released at the end of the war.

Desmond Doss was a conscientious objector and would not carry a rifle; but as an Army medic, he rescued wounded men from under withering enemy fire and protected them even though he was wounded worse than some of them. The President awarded him the Medal of Honor.

While flying with VMF-221 Marine Squadron, **Lieutenant Jim Swett** shot down seven Japanese planes one right after the other. A Japanese rear gunner then shot him down, and he crashed at sea. His only injury was a broken nose. He was rescued by a picket boat (destroyer escort used as early-warning ships), and ended up with 15 Japanese planes to his credit. He also received the Medal of Honor.

Lieutenant Frank Holmes was at Pearl Harbor the day it was bombed. That night he had to stand guard duty at our only remaining operational airfield. Later he went to Guadalcanal and flew P-38s. On 18 April 1943, he was on the mission that shot down Admiral Yamamoto, and he himself shot down a Zero and a bomber.

Marine **Major Bruce Porter**, flying an F4U Corsair and later an F6F Hellcat, shot down five planes, two on night missions. He obviously had excellent communications with his ground control intercept (GCI) operator.

Lieutenant Joe Robbins of the U.S. Navy flew F6Fs and later F4Us. The F6F was an excellent dive bomber and fighter plane. It could carry two 1,000-pound bombs. In May 1945, when the Japanese were using kamikaze planes against our ships with deadly accuracy at Okinawa, he shot down four in one mission.

Ensign Harry Swinburn landed his badly shot-up Hellcat on the aircraft carrier USS *Hornet II* at night — a miraculous feat. He later shot down six planes and also sank a freighter.

Ensign Spider Webb got seven victories, most of them in one day. His plane was badly shot up, but he made it back to the carrier.

Lieutenant Wendell VanTwelves shot down 13. Two were Zeroes that were attacking our floatplanes as they were picking up downed pilots in the water. The Japanese had wasted our floatplanes, but the Lieutenant saved our boys' lives by providing cover until they were picked up by our submarines.

EARLIER IN THE BOOK I spoke of the American Volunteer Group (AVG) Flying Tigers formed in 1941 by General Claire Lee Chennault in China and their efforts against the Japanese. Their kill ratio was 12 Japanese planes to one P-40. The mission of the AVGs was to control the Burma Road and keep it open for supplies to come through Burma from India to China. Without these supplies, China would soon fold up. These Flying Tigers were hired by Chiang Kai-shek's Chinese government. The commander was Colonel Robert L. Scott, who is credited with 22 kills while commanding the 23rd Fighter Squadron. Tex Hill also was a leader.

The largest mission General Chennault ever put together was 14 bombers and 22 P-40 fighters, against which the Japanese sent up 45 fighters. The AVGs shot down 29 of them, and our bombers destroyed a loaded ship carrying aircraft and supplies. The AVG lost no planes on that strike.

On 20 August 1942, Marine Squadron VMF-121 landed with 19 F4F fighter planes and pilots on Henderson Field on Guadalcanal. **Captain Joe Foss** was placed in command. In 63 days, he shot down 26 Japanese airplanes. The Japanese Navy soon retaliated, shelling Foss's base with 18- and 14-inch guns. They nearly destroyed it, wiping out many planes and destroying nearly all of the gasoline, ammunition, and other supplies. After desperate fighting by our troops on the ground, our men in the air, and our ships, the tide began to turn. Guadalcanal was a "busy and exposed" place.

Captain Marion Carl's squadron VMF-223 suffered nearly a 43 percent casualty rate, but they shot down 93 enemy fighters and bombers. Later, as a test pilot, Captain Carl for a time held the world's speed and altitude records.

The Marine Air Corps shot down a total of 2,439 aircraft despite the fact that the Japanese Zero could outfly and outmaneuver the F4F. The Marines later got F4U Corsairs, which turned out to be one of the best fighter aircraft of the war.

Early in the war in the Pacific, the Japanese bomber formations were so strict and rigid that they would not break formation, so it was relatively easy for our fighters to pick them off one at a time. They did not take any evasive action. Sometimes this is good; sometimes this is bad. Our own large bombers also stayed in formation, so that they could concentrate their gun power from their turrets on a fighter plane.

THE NAVY DESTROYED 6,826 planes of the Rising Sun. The Navy's leading ace was **Ike Kepford**, who shot down 17 Japanese planes. **Tom Blackburn** shot down 11 while commanding VF-17, the Navy's best fighter squadron. VF-17 lost 12 pilots, but knocked down 152 total planes. Best of all, none of the ships Blackburn was covering was ever hit by a bomb or a torpedo, and none of the bombers he was escorting were ever shot down by an enemy plane.

Lieutenant Commander Butch O'Hare intercepted nine Japanese twin-engine bombers about to attack the aircraft carrier USS *Lexington*. He shot down five and damaged a sixth. For this, President Roosevelt awarded him the Medal of Honor in April 1942, when our country really needed a boost. Sixteen out of the 18 enemy bombers were shot down in that skirmish. O'Hare Field (now O'Hare International Airport) in Chicago was named for him. In November 1943, he was commanding Navy Squadron VF-6 and flying the F6F Hellcat when he was shot down. It was never revealed whether or not the cause was friendly fire, with one of our own gunners firing on him by mistake, or an unseen enemy, who slipped in and then slipped away. The downing occurred at night, and night flying increased the risks and odds against a pilot.

The U.S. Army Air Corps shot down 5,214 Japanese aircraft. The 475th Fighter Group of the 5th Air Force, in the South Pacific, was an all-P-38 group that alone shot down 551 planes.

Chapter 9

Why the Atomic Bomb?

IN APRIL 1945, when Vice President Truman became President, we were developing the atomic bomb. We didn't know how much death and destruction it would reap. It is said that the President agonized over whether or not to drop this mighty weapon on Japan. At that time, our bombers were destroying targets and cities with fire and demolition bombs throughout Japan.

On 2 July 1945, we made a direct appeal by radio for Japan to surrender or face total destruction. Tokyo replied that it did not like the terms of unconditional surrender, then formally rejected the offer.

On 23 July 1945, 1,000 carrier-based planes and 600 B-29s rained more bombs on Japan.

On 6 August 1945, President Truman announced to the world that we had dropped an atomic bomb on Hiroshima; on 8 August, a second one was dropped on Nagasaki. That same day, Russia declared war on Japan.

On 14 August, Japan announced its surrender. The Allies allowed Japan to keep her Emperor. On 2 September 1945, formal surrender papers were signed aboard the battleship USS *Missouri*. General Wainwright, who had been a prisoner of the Japanese for over three years after his surrender on Corregidor and in very poor health, was invited to sign. I believe that he honorably represented his men, both living and dead, and all those who had struggled against Japanese cruelty and aggression.

A Japanese delegation signed for Emperor Hirohito, who was not present. When General Douglas MacArthur signed, he assumed full and complete power over Japan. The Emperor was allowed to stay on the throne, but in name only.

In the end, I believe we were more than generous to those countries that had caused this great conflict. I wrote the following article which appeared in the *Arizona Range News* (Willcox) on Wednesday, 13 September 1995, and which is graciously reprinted here by permission of the editor.

My View on the Dropping of the Atomic Bomb

by W. M. Gaskill

Special to the *Arizona Range News*

I believe our scholars and historians do not have an intimate knowledge of a most important part of our country's history. Many evidently did not have any friends, loved ones or family members who were killed or maimed by the Japanese in World War II; beginning with the sneak attack on Pearl Harbor.

The Japanese attacked us and killed over 2,400 Americans and sank most of our Navy in that area. Following this was the invasion and overthrowing of the Philippines and the brutal treatment of thousands of American and Philippino [*sic*] soldiers and civilians who became prisoners of the Japanese.

The Japanese had already taken over Manchuria, part of

China, much of Southeast Asia and the South Pacific. The Imperial Japanese Army and Navy were on the way to capture Australia and New Zealand.

Not only did they strike us first, but their extreme cruelty to all of their captives must be stressed. Our young people must be told about this by those who know first hand.

President Truman and Prime Minister Churchill decided to drop the atomic bomb on Hiroshima which killed 70,000 people (some estimates say up to 140,000 killed). Three days later we dropped another bomb on Nagasaki, killing 40,000 people.

For those who question the morality of dropping the big bomb maybe we should all study some of the realities of World War II. The Japanese believed that to die for their country was glorious; to surrender was cowardly. This was evidenced by the fact that we would sometimes only capture one prisoner out of a thousand. The rest would prefer to fight on until they were killed or they committed suicide. In the case at Biak I saw (and smelled) where they preferred to be incinerated by a flame thrower rather than give up. This was true in Guam, Saipan, Iwo Jima and many other islands.

Another thing, the Japanese soldiers at that time were so cruel to their captives (soldiers or civilians) and they tortured, bayoneted, hung or beheaded the prisoners for the slightest provocation.

In the Philippines they withheld water or food for punishment. They would kill several prisoners in retaliation for every one that escaped. If they caught the escapee his head would be impaled on the prison fence for all to see.

Most of our men who fought in the trenches, so to speak, and survived believe that had we invaded Japan the Japanese would have dug into the mountains and fought until almost the very last one was killed rather than surrender. It would have been a terrible slaughter on both sides.

As it was, the two bombs were such a psychological shock that the Emperor of Japan decided to give up. We later found out that the Japanese still had seven million soldiers in reserve. This was more than twice what we thought they had. They even had six to nine thousand planes hidden away awaiting the invasion. If they would have used them in suicide attacks one can only guess what they would have cost us in lives and ships.

A memo written to President Truman from General George Marshall states that in planning for the invasion the planners refer to the potential loss of life to be from 500,000 to one million or more of our men, most of this being in the first 30 days.

Linda Goetz Holmes, author of "Four Thousand Bowls of Rice" discovered while checking in the Japanese military papers in the National Archives this order from the Japanese high command to its commandants of all Prisoner of War Camps — "It is the aim to annihilate them all and not leave any traces." There were 100,000 prisoners being held in Japanese Prisoner of War Camps which were released at the end of the war.

I believe that dropping the atomic bombs [*was*] terrible, but in the end it probably save[*d*] millions of lives on both sides.

I was disheartened to read that the Smithsonian . . . exhibited 49 photos of suffering Japanese survivors of the A-bomb and only three photos of suffering Americans and downplayed the casualty estimates for the U.S. invasion that were given to President Truman.

They talked about anti-Asian racism but did not mention much about what the Japanese did on Pearl Harbor and following.

The Smithsonian, of all people, neglects to tell the whole story; the thousands upon thousands of Chinese men, women and children whom the Japanese murdered; the death march of Philippine and American soldiers in 1942; the terrible atrocities against Prisoners of War throughout the war; the slave labor, and on and on.

Some of our history teachers should be survivors and veterans and have first hand knowledge of how it really was. That way, our leaders of tomorrow would not have some watered down misleading information about a most important event.

Young people will need to have accurate information in order that they may be able to make wise decisions in the future.

The "Scholars" suggest that the casualty figures projected following an invasion of Japan are preposterous. "Get real" guys. Many of those Japanese people had no intention of ever giving up. Our scholars also believe it was a vengeful act on our part. Well, all wars have some of that.

Sooner or later the big bomb was going to be dropped by someone. Germany was well on its way to having this bomb. What do you think Germany and Japan would have done with it?

Make no mistake about it — President Truman made the right decision, although I imagine it grieved him deeply. General Curtis LeMay said that the business of war is killing and when enough people have been killed the war ceases. This may be brutal but that is the way it is.

Chapter 10

A Last Word

T*HE COMPLETE HISTORY OF WORLD WAR II,* by Francis Trevelyan Miller (1945), states that in the last 3,000 years, 12 out of every 13 years have seen a war going on. It was to this end that President Roosevelt, in 1941, advocated four human freedoms to all nations:

1. Freedom of speech and expression throughout the world.
2. Freedom to worship god.
3. Freedom from want.
4. Freedom from fear.

Today, over 50 years after World War II, wars continue; the dream of world peace fades. Technology provides more advanced ways of waging war, but not much in the way of waging peace. This is a sad commentary on the human race.

Historians believe that World War II continued the unfinished World War I, that the Nazis and Japanese had planned to take away all freedoms, destroy the church, and set up a slavery system to be ruled by a "Master Race." Germany, Italy, and Japan — the Axis — had formed an economic and political alliance. Japan demanded that we stop aid to China's Chiang Kai-shek.

I notice that some history books have left out the fact that when Pearl Harbor was attacked on 7 December 1941 the United States already had sent many of our National Guard Troops from different states, converted to the 200th and 515th Coast Battalions, to the Philippines with no back-up. Immediately following the disastrous raid, the Japanese wiped out our Marines on Wake Island and Guam, then attacked the Philippines, the Malay peninsula, and many other islands in the Pacific.

President Roosevelt's aim and his promise to keep us out of the war were shattered. Our Armed Services were at a very low level, and we were caught totally unprepared. We then sent aid to Britain, and still nothing to help our boys in the Philippines. It was months before we could gather enough naval strength to even begin to confront the Japanese fleet, the air and sea armadas that stormed into Manila, which was almost leveled by Japanese bombers.

In May 1942, as General MacArthur and his wife and son were smuggled out of Bataan, leaving General Wainwright in charge, our troops had completely run out of food, medicine, and supplies and had to surrender to the Japanese. Within a few months, the latter had overrun the Philippines, Thailand, the Malay peninsula, Singapore, and the Dutch East Indies, as well as hundreds of other little islands, and were on their way to Australia and New Zealand. I have repeated this in order to stress the fact that we were caught so unprepared militarily, and we don't want to ever be found that way again.

Many figures about World War II have been presented in different books. These statistics vary greatly; some are double others on a particular item. Who knows which source is most accurate!

During World War II, 15,000,000 Americans served in the Armed Forces, 10,000,000 in the Army alone.

Over 360,000 of our young men and women were killed on all fronts of the war.

Russia had the most casualties, followed by Germany, Poland, and China. Polish civilians suffered millions of casualties at the hands of both Germany and Russia. Germany lost about an equal number of civilians and military.

There were about six million Jews killed by the Nazis.

This was the largest, most costly war ever fought, both in number of lives lost and cost of materiél.

The total loss of lives is estimated to be about 50,000,000 people.

Francis Miller's estimates of World War II death losses follow (*The Complete History of World War II*):

Country	Military	Civilian	Total
Russia	13,300,000	7,000,000	20,300,000
Germany	3,250,000	3,600,000	6,850,000
Poland	600,000	6,000,000	6,600,000
China		6,000,000	6,000,000
Japan	2,000,000	1,000,000	3,000,000
Yugoslavia	300,000	1,300,000	1,600,000
Romania	200,000	465,000	665,000
France	250,000	360,000	610,000
British Empire			484,482
Greece			420,000
Italy	330,000	80,000	410,000
Hungary	120,000	280,000	400,000
United States	362,561		362,561
Czechoslovakia	10,000	330,000	340,000
Australia	27,000		27,000
Finland			27,000

It is estimated that nearly a quarter of a million slave laborers from China, Burma, the Malay states, and other islands died at the hands of Japanese guards. The "Death Railway" in Burma took another 50,000 Allied prisoners; they were killed by overwork, starvation, disease, cruelty, and murder. I won't go into the figures and descriptions of the cruelty inflicted by Russians and Germans against humanity — Jews, Gypsies, and political dissidents; that is a whole other book. Millions of people were scarred mentally and physically for the rest of their lives. Millions died with no record of who they were or where they were from — forever to remain unknown.

At the beginning of World War II, United States retaliation against Japan was on a pitifully small scale. Even the Doolittle raid on Tokyo that surprised the world was only a drop in the bucket of what was to come. The 16 B-25s, carrying one ton of bombs each, were a wonderful and heroic feat that really woke up the Japanese to the realization that their homeland was vulnerable. However, the material damage done was almost negligible in comparison with what happened as the war progressed.

Even when I arrived on the scene, we thought a few Japanese bombed, or a barge blown up, or a fuel dump exploded was a huge success. The foot soldiers were successful when they had gained only a few feet of ground at a time, or when a few enemy planes were shot down, or a ship sunk. But toward the end of the war, B-29 Superfortresses dropped 169,000 tons of bombs on Japan. One bombing raid on Tokyo reportedly killed 97,000 people in the fire storm that followed; then came the atomic bombs that brought about the end of the war.

Although I dive bombed and strafed supply depots, shipping, and other military installations, and also did my job as a test pilot, I deeply regretted having missed all that aerial combat. However, a sobering thought comes to mind — I am here to write about this when well over 350,000 of our men did not return and hundreds of thousands more were wounded. Millions of people throughout the world are alive and free today because of the victorious Allies. Had the Nazis or the Japanese been victors, they would have shown no mercy at all.

I was proud of our country then. I am proud of it now, although we have made some terrible mistakes.

I should fall on my knees daily and thank God for having been spared and for my family, my friends, and my country.

South Pacific Album

Bill Gaskill.

GENERAL ORDERS)
:
NO. 593)

HEADQUARTERS
FAR EAST AIR FORCES
APO 925 - 22 April 1945.

EXTRACT

AIR MEDAL (OAK-LEAF CLUSTER) - Awards

Section
III

* * * * *

III. AIR MEDAL (OAK-LEAF CLUSTER). By direction of the President, in additin to the Air Medal awarded to the following named officers by the Commanding General, USAFISPA, as published in General Orders No. 435, Headquarters, USAFISPA, 27 March 1944, Bronze Oak-Leaf Clusters are awarded to them by the Commanding General, Far East Air Forces, under the provisions of Executive Order No. 9158, 11 May 1942 (Bulletin 25, WD, 1942), as amended by Executive Order No. 9242-A, 11 September 1942 (Bulletin 49, WD, 1942).

1. EIGHTH OAK-LEAF CLUSTER.

First Lieutenant WALTER I. OLSON, (O801897). Air Corps, United States Army. For operational flight missions from 18 August 1944 to 9 November 1944. Home address: Mrs. Myrtle Hubson (Sister), Greenbush, Minn.

2. TENTH OAK-LEAF CLUSTER.

First Lieutenant WILLIAM M. GASKILL, (O804149). Air Corps, United States Army. For operational flight missions from 18 August 1944 to 6 November 1944. Home address: Mrs. Elvena F. Gaskill (Wife), Box 63, Deming, N.M.

The citation is as follows:

For meritorious achievement while participating in sustained operational flight missions in the Southwest Pacific Area during which hostile contact was probable and expected. These operations included escorting bombers and transport aircraft, interception and attack missions, and patrol and reconnaissance flights. In the course of these operations, strafing and bombing attacks were made from dangerously low altitudes, destroying and damaging enemy installations and equipment. The courage and devotion to duty displayed during these flights are worthy of commendation.

* * * * *

/s/ George C. Kenney.
/t/ GEORGE C. KENNEY,
General, United States Army,
Commanding.

A TRUE EXTRACT COPY:
John L. DeArmond
JOHN L. DE ARMOND,
1st Lt., Air Corps,
Awards Officer.

GENERAL ORDERS)
:
No. 88)

HEADQUARTERS
FAR EAST AIR FORCES
APO 925 - 13 January 1945

EXTRACT

III. AIR MEDAL OAK LEAF CLUSTER. By direction of the President, in addition to the Air Medal ~~awarded to First Lieutenant~~ WILLIAM M. GASKILL by the Commanding General, USAFISPA, as published in General Orders No. 435, Headquarters USAFISPA, 27 March 1944, a fourth Bronze Oak-Leaf Cluster is awarded to him by the Commanding General, Far East Air Forces, under the provisions of Executive Order No. 9158, 11 May 1942 (Bulletin 25, WD. 1942), as amended by Executive Order No. 9242-A, 11 September 1942 (Bulletin 49, WD, 1942). The citation is as follows:

First Lieutenant WILLIAM M. GASKILL, (0804149), Air Corps, United States Army. For meritorious achievement while participating in an aerial flight to Tarakan, Borneo, on 18 November 1944. This officer was the pilot of one of a formation of twenty-six P-38 aircraft which took off for an incendiary bombing and strafing mission against oil fields at this Japanese base. After flying six-hundred miles, the formation dropped to an altitude of 200 feet. As they approached the target, some of the aircraft made minimum-altitude runs over assigned targets while others flew top-cover. In the face of intense anti-aircraft fire a successful attack was made which set fire to numerous tanks, three merchant vessels, a tanker, three small vessels under construction, nine or ten barges and small boats in the harbor, a pumping station and other installations. Flames and smoke rose to a height of 17,000 feet, and fires and explosions were in evidence for three days. The courage and devotion to duty displayed by Lieutenant Gaskill in the partial destruction of this vital enemy oil source are worthy of commendation.
Home address: Mrs. Elvena F. Gaskill, (Wife), Box 63, Deming, N. Mex.

/s/ George C. Kenney,
/t/ GEORGE C. KENNEY,
Lieutenant General, U. S., Army
Commanding.

A TRUE EXTRACT COPY:
John L. De Armond
JOHN L. DE ARMOND
1st Lt., Air Corps.

HEADQUARTERS
FAR EAST AIR FORCES
APO 925 - 1 February 1945

GENERAL ORDERS)
:
No. 203)

EXTRACT

* * * * * * *

VI. SOLDIERS' MEDAL. By direction of the President, under the provisions of t act of congress approved 2 July 1926 (Bulletin 8, WD, 1926), a Soldier's Medal is awarded by the Commanding General, Far East Air Forces, to the following named officers:

First Lieutenant WILLIAM H. GASKILL, (O804149), Air Corps, United States Army.

Home address: Mrs. Elvena F. Gaskill (Wife), Box 63, Deming, N. Mex.

The Citation is as follows:

For heroism at Tarakan, Borneo, Netherlands East Indies, on 21 and 22 November 1944. When bad weather cancelled a scheduled search for a missing pilot, these officers volunteered for the mission. Arriving at Tarakan, the four P-38's piloted by these officers, split and searched individually for the downed pilot, who was finally discovered fifty miles to the south. They were forced to return to base because of fuel shortage, but there they secured a PBY and escorted it back through a severe tropical front in order to pick up the lost pilot. Nearly all of the flight to Borneo and back had to be accomplished on instruments. The heroism displayed by these officers reflects great credit on themselves and the Military Service.

* * * * *

/s/ George C. Kenney
/t/ GEORGE C. KENNEY
Lieutenant General, U S Army
Commanding

A TRUE EXTRACT COPY: John L. DeArmond
JOHN L. DE ARMOND
1st Lt., Air Corps.

Above, l to r: McBride, Love, Grooms, Gaskill, ____, 68th Fighter Squadron.

Russ Schafer.

Right: R. Love.

Lester R. Leidy.

Left: Fred Roos.

Our flight surgeon, Captain "Doc" Krielkamp, Sydney, Australia.

Middleburg Island, December 1944. Circled area is the point where the men watched planes take off.

U.S. POSTAGE
VIA AIR MAIL
6¢
U.S. ARMY POSTAL SERVICE
JUL 17
3 PM
1944
To:
Mrs. William M. Gaskill
Box 817
Deming New Mexico
U.S.A.
AIR MAIL

Index

by Lori L. Daniel